UNDER OPEN SKY

BOOKS BY NORBERT KRAPF

The Playfair Book of Hours (1976)
Finding the Grain: Pioneer Journals, Franconian Folktales, Ancestral Poems
(1977)
Arriving on Paumanok (1979)
Lines Drawn from Dürer (1981)
Heartwood (1983)
Circus Songs (1984)
A Dream of Plum Blossoms (1985)
East of New York City (1986)
Under Open Sky: Poets on William Cullen Bryant (1986)

UNDER OPEN SKY

Poets on William Cullen Bryant

EDITED BY NORBERT KRAPF

WOOD ENGRAVINGS BY JOHN DE POL

FORDHAM UNIVERSITY PRESS
NEW YORK · MCMLXXXVI

Reprinted from the original edition by The Stone House Press.

Library of Congress Card Number: 86-61717

ISBN 0-8232-1167-3 (clothbound)
ISBN 0-8232-1168-1 (paperback)

Printed in the United States of America

for Vince Clemente,
friend of poets and poetry

❧

CONTENTS

CONTENTS

II. Underground Tide: Poems

Bryant pulsing the first interior verse-throbs of a mighty world — bard of the river and the wood, ever conveying a taste of open air, with scents as from hay-fields, grapes, birch-borders — always lurkingly fond of threnodies — beginning and ending his long career with chants of death, with here and there through all, poems, or passages of poems, touching the highest universal truths, enthusiasms, duties — morals as grim and eternal, if not as stormy and fateful, as anything in Eschylus.

— Walt Whitman, *Specimen Days*

To me it seems that one of the most important requisites for a great poet is a luminous style. The elements of poetry lie in natural objects, in the vicissitudes of human life, in the emotions of the human heart, and the relations of man to man. He who can present them in combinations and lights which at once affect the mind with a deep sense of their truth and beauty is the poet for his own age and the ages that succeed it. It is no disparagement either to his skill or his power that he finds them near at hand; the nearer they lie to the common track of human intelligence, the more certain he is of the sympathy of his own generation, and of those which shall come after him.

— William Cullen Bryant, "Introduction," *A Library of Poetry and Song*

ACKNOWLEDGMENTS

Jared Carter's "Raccoon Grove" originally appeared in *Images*, © 1984 Jared Carter. William Heyen's "Downriver" was written for the sesquicentennial of the city of Rochester, New York, first read on 28 April 1984 at opening ceremonies in the Eastman Theatre, and appeared in *Upstate*, © 1984 William Heyen. John Hollander's "William Cullen Bryant as Poet" originally appeared as the "Introduction" to the Chelsea House reissue of the John Bigelow biography *William Cullen Bryant* in the American Men of Letters Series, © 1980 Chelsea House. Norbert Krapf's "Walking with Walt Whitman and William Cullen Bryant: A Fantasy," originally appeared, without the subtitle, in *West Hills Review* and was included in his *Arriving on Paumanok* (Street Press), © 1979 Norbert Krapf. Norbert Krapf's "William Cullen Bryant's Roslyn Poems," based on the longer lecture/article "An Invitation to the Country: William Cullen Bryant in Roslyn," published in *Ventures in Research*, 8 (1979), edited by Richard Griffith (C. W. Post Center, Long Island University, 1981), appeared with its present title, but in a shortened version, in the anthology *Paumanok Rising*, edited by Vince Clemente and Graham Everett (Street Press, 1981), © 1981 Norbert Krapf. William Jay Smith's "Winter Morning" originally appeared in *The New Yorker* and was included in his *The Traveler's Tree: New and Selected Poems* (Persea Books), © 1980 William Jay Smith. Thanks to the poets and their publishers for permission to reprint these materials.

The editor wishes to thank the trustees of Long Island University for the 1984–85 sabbatical that facilitated the completion of this book.

INTRODUCTION

PERHAPS THIS GATHERING of writings by contemporary American poets about William Cullen Bryant originated when I moved to Roslyn in 1974 after a year of teaching in England. I had moved away from my native Indiana to Long Island in 1970, a few months before I began to write poetry. Without knowing it, for three years every winter I passed within view of Bryant's Cedarmere along Hempstead Bay on my way to teach American literature classes at the C. W. Post Campus of Long Island University. Those three years, however, my imagination was taken with the rural Midwest I had left behind, not with suburban Long Island. When I moved to Roslyn, where the past is everywhere visible, I wrote my first poems set on Long Island. By the time my wife and I bought a small old house on Main Street in 1977, I was well on my way to completing the slim volume *Arriving on Paumanok*. Walt Whitman had been influencing the way I was seeing contemporary Long Island; and William Cullen Bryant, who also arrived in Roslyn from elsewhere, was becoming part of my daily landscape. My eyes were opening.

As we settled into our old house, I explored the subject of Bryant's life in, and writings about, Roslyn for what I thought might become a book. That project yielded instead a thirty-page lecture-article titled "An Invitation to the Country: William Cullen Bryant in Roslyn," condensed here by more than half to the essay on Bryant's Roslyn poems. As I learned more about Bryant's accomplishments as a man of letters and citizen of the community, nation, and world, as I entered and re-entered his poems with students at Long Island University and the University of Freiburg in Germany, I projected a cycle of poems about Bryant at Cedarmere that never seemed to materialize.

In the spring of 1984, William Stafford was scheduled to read his poetry on campus at the annual Poetry Awards Night. Shortly before he was to leave Oregon, I came across a photocopy of my Bryant article, scribbled a note saying the essay might prepare him for his visit to Roslyn, and mailed it to the Kansas-born poet. He surprised me by showing up bright and early one April morning, the day before I expected him, so that we would have time to visit the "Bryant sites" together. He quietly offered his opinion that more people should have the chance to learn the forgotten story of Bryant the man and his poetry. The day after Stafford left I wrote "By the Waters of Cedarmere" and conceived the idea of a book of writings by fellow poets about this once-famous poet. Stafford replied to my letter about the proposal with the first of two fine poems he sent.

Morris Gelfand, who operates the Stone House Press out of the basement of a house Bryant had built in Roslyn, and who had published my *Heartwood* collection of poems about trees, offered to publish a letterpress limited edition of the Bryant book. For technical reasons, I was to be limited to no more than 150 pages and 20 poets. Of the writings collected here, only the John Hollander essay, the Jared Carter, William Heyen, and William Jay Smith poems, and my prose fantasy and critical essay have been previously published. Aaron Kramer's essay is a transcript, with minor revisions, of a radio broadcast he gave in 1978.

In inviting poets to contribute, I followed my instincts about which contemporary poets, as revealed by their poems and comments about poetry, might be receptive to, though not necessarily uncritical of, Bryant's poetry. Stressing space limitations and the need for brevity, I explained that I would be open to poems and short prose pieces, in any form and with any approach, in response to Bryant's poetry and/or any other aspect of his multifaceted life and career. I indicated that I would be receptive to negative criticism, if it seemed just; Bryant was too dedicated a poet and too principled a man to be patronized. If we ultimately find him to be a "minor" poet, we must realize that it is indeed no mean accomplishment to be a minor poet. Unfortunately, we live in a world in which the poems of even "major" poets go largely unread.

I have arranged the poems and prose pieces by twenty contemporary American poets into two sections titled by phrases from a Robert Morgan essay and a William Stafford poem. The poets are of several generations and at different stages of their careers as poets, ranging from those who appear in little magazines and journals but are awaiting the publication of their first volumes, to those whose distinguished lists of collections have earned them prestigious awards and international recognition. In this book and elsewhere, they write in a typically American diversity of styles, forms, and traditions. What has brought them together, above and beyond my persistence, is an eagerness to respond to the voice, vision, and legacy of a literary ancestor who, though once nationally and internationally acclaimed, is now remarkably out of fashion. If I had been given more space, I am sure other poets would have wanted to join in the dialogue.

As John Hollander observes, today we do not consider Bryant the equal of Emerson, Whitman, and Dickinson. In his day, however, he was thought preeminent. On his 70th birthday in 1864, the Century Club honored him with a gala celebration, a portfolio of paintings by distinguished artists, and tributes by Emerson, Dana, Lowell, Whittier, Holmes, Longfellow and Tuckerman. A little over 120 years later, the time is right for a reconsideration of Bryant's merits as a poet. Under the superb editorship of William Cullen Bryant II, four of a projected six volumes of Bryant's letters have been published. A collection of scholarly essays, *William Cullen Bryant and His America*, appeared a few years ago. Bryant's Cedarmere home in Roslyn Harbor will soon be opened to the public. We have been hearing from Bryant again in his fascinating letters, we have heard from scholars, and now it is time to hear from our poets as they reflect, sometimes darkly, on Bryant from the perspective of our time.

In the blank-verse meditation "Thanatopsis," the poem most often referred to in this book, Bryant advised:

> When thoughts
> Of the last bitter hour come like a blight
> Over thy spirit, and sad images
> Of the stern agony, and shroud, and pall,
> And breathless darkness, and the narrow house,
> Make thee to shudder, and grow sick at heart; —
> Go forth, under the open sky, and list
> To Nature's teachings, while from all around —
> Earth and her waters, and the depths of air —
> Comes a still voice . . .

Whether we find ourselves under an open sky or in the classroom, in a library or at home, it is time for us to re-open our eyes and ears and listen to Bryant's "still voice." Walt Whitman's singling out of Bryant as our first significant poet of nature and death, and as purveyor of dark moral truths, is echoed in a number of these reflections by contemporary American poets. As they arrived here in Roslyn, these poems and prose pieces opened my eyes and ears further. I hope they also open the minds and hearts of many a reader.

—*Norbert Krapf*
Roslyn, Long Island

Forest Shadows:

Prose

NORBERT KRAPF

William Cullen Bryant's Roslyn Poems

WHEN WILLIAM CULLEN BRYANT bought "forty acres of solid earth" in Hempstead Harbor (soon to be renamed Roslyn) in 1843, he was an important figure in the cultural and political life of New York City. In 1825 he had abandoned his law practice in the Western Massachusetts town of Great Barrington and come to the metropolis to make his living as a man of letters. By then he was already known in literary circles as the author of "Thanatopsis," a breakthrough poem which had appeared in *The North American Review* in 1817, the 1821 Phi Beta Kappa poem "The Ages," and a critically acclaimed first collection, *Poems*, published that same year. He came to New York as the editor of a new literary review, but a few years after he arrived in the city his career took an unexpected turn. He became editor-in-chief of the *Evening Post*, an established and prosperous newspaper. Under Bryant's editorship, which lasted for over fifty years, the paper became even more influential, prestigious, and prosperous. Eventually, Bryant was freed of all financial worries. He came to his summers in Roslyn a well-traveled political journalist, an internationally respected poet, and an aggressive champion of the arts. It has been said that he set up his "half country life" in Roslyn, as he called it, to escape from the pressures of life and work in the city, a view Bryant encourages in his letters; but the impulse simply to return to the country must have been equally strong in the man who in his seventies would write so movingly in an aborted "auto-biography" of his childhood in the foothills of the Berkshires.

In coming to Roslyn, Bryant was on some level returning, or trying to return, to the rural landscape of his youth. The urge to reach back to one's childhood, which Rainer Maria Rilke described as "that precious kingly possession, that treasure house of memories," is of course universal. As Allan Seager said of Theodore Roethke in *The Glass House*, "The first definitions, the fruits of the primary glances, can never be supplanted, for the trees of one's childhood are the touchstones of all later trees." When Bryant looked at the hilly woods on the farm he was to buy in Hempstead Harbor, he must have seen the Massachusetts forests which inspired "Thanatopsis," "Inscription for the Entrance to a Wood," and "A Forest Hymn." It is not surprising that in an early Roslyn poem, "The Unknown Way," he looks at the steep hill east of his Quaker farmhouse and refers to "mountains."

The landscape in several poems, together with the repeatedly idyllic vignettes in the letters, reveals that Roslyn did indeed serve Bryant as a refuge from the gloomy, noisy city where he earned his fortune as newspaper editor and owner. His letters to close friends often hum with lyrical invitations to the country. A good example is the one to his poet friend Richard Henry Dana Sr. written on July 4, 1850:

> I have been passing a few days at my place on Long Island, and tomorrow must go back to the town — the foul, hot noisy town. How it will smell of the tons of gunpowder that have been burnt in it today! I hear the thunder of its guns even here, but it does not disturb the birds. The fire-bird and the song-sparrow have been singing all day among my locusts and horse-chestnuts, in spite of it. We have quite given the world the go-by to-day. We have been no farther than the garden, from the foot of which we saw in the morning a sloop go down the bay, with a fiddle on board, and a score of young women in sun-bonnets. Nobody has been to see us but a little boy of two years old, whom, at his particular desire, I took to the barn to see the pigs and chickens, and whom I was obliged to refresh with a liberal handful of cherries which I climbed the tree to gather. Between eleven and twelve o'clock I had rather a sweltering time in the garden gathering the first of the raspberries and the last of the strawberries. . . .

Throughout the thirty-five years that Bryant maintained a country home in Roslyn, his vigorous support of the arts in New York City involved him in many causes and kept him in contact with many distinguished writers, artists, architects, and politicians. Although Bryant knew the most illustrious people of his age, he invited only a select few into the circle of his country life in Roslyn. A public figure who cultivated his privacy, Bryant expresses his need to share his life on Long Island in a poem he wrote to his favorite daughter, Julia. In "An Invitation to the Country," Bryant describes the signs of spring that are evident around "our summer dwelling," the Easter sparrow, a bluebird chanting in the elm, a south wind. He then interrupts the rural vision with an urgent invitation: "Come, daughter mine, from the gloomy city,/Before those lays from the elm have ceased." Country life had to be shared with friends and family in order to be fully enjoyed. Bryant may have been a private man, as his biographers like to tell us, but he was not selfish. He knew how to share what he had earned through his labors as a journalist.

The bucolic vision also informs "A Rain-Dream," a blank-verse fantasy about the beauties of the rural landscape after a refreshing rain. Here the invitation to the country becomes almost an exhortation:

> Let us awhile
> As the slow wind is rolling up the storm,
> In fancy leave this maze of dusty streets,
> Forever shaken by the importunate jar
> Of commerce, and upon the darkening air
> Look from the shelter of our rural home.

As antidote to urban blight, Bryant prescribes the woods, hills, fields, cottages, and local flora and fauna as they appear after a purifying rain.

Not all the Roslyn poems, however, are so idyllic. In several poems Bryant enters what seems to be an unfamiliar world and approaches the mysteries which he senses lie beyond the familiar. "The Unknown Way," one of the first poems Bryant wrote in Roslyn, is a heavily allegorical piece about the journey of life which takes off from a "dusty path" that "opens/Eastward" into the woods. Without suggesting an answer, Bryant finally asks whether the path will "clamber the bald mountainside" or end "where the waters roar."

In a letter Bryant once told a friend how much he enjoyed laying out paths in the woods above his farmhouse and clearing views of the bay below. As we might expect, Bryant left thirty acres of woodlands (his property in Roslyn gradually increased to almost 200 acres) on the hillside east of his house. "The Path" begins with two stanzas describing the pleasure it gave Bryant to work in these woods while his wife watched at his side. The poem then changes from realistic observation to abstract meditation on the effects a path has on the wilderness. A rather eighteenth-century sense of order, perhaps derived from Bryant's early reading of Neoclassical authors, is imposed upon the scene; as a result the wilderness becomes "homelike" or domesticated, and the swamp turns into a "garden with strange flowers and sprays." Bryant tries to convince us of the universality of rural life: archetypal maids with their buckets, laborers and schoolboys and Sunday worshippers and mourners and matrons and travelers all appear on the allegorical path before it enters cities and joins East and West and, implausibly, leaps to the shores of "the great deep."

In "The Tides," a much better poem than "The Unknown Way" or "The Path," the sea becomes a mysterious presence in Bryant's vision. The sea of this poem is not the "still" and pond-like Sound in which Bryant, as he frequently wrote friends, enjoyed his thera-

peutic "sea-bathing." In "The Tides," Bryant's imagination trans-
forms the local scene into an image of limitation and imprisonment.
A poem of nocturnal silence, it begins with an announcement that
no voice speaks "from the great woodlands round." Instead, the
speaker hears the heaving and moaning of "the restless Deep." He
hears, in the sounds of the sea, a struggling, complaining, and
longing to escape its boundaries. A powerful but unspecified yearn-
ing for release can be felt in the imagery.

Several poems on subjects literally closer to home – about activ-
ities around the farm, mainly gardening – give us a more direct
view of Bryant's life in Roslyn. There is no doubt that the garden
was the center of Bryant's life as a country gentleman. Contemporary
magazines like *Hearth and Home, Appleton's Journal, Scribner's
Monthly,* and *Moore's Rural Life* give graphic descriptions of the
gardens. Bryant loved to experiment with fruits. He had different
varieties of gooseberries, strawberries, blackberries, currants, and
grapes, of which he grew some twenty varieties. The south front of
his barns and sheds were draped with grapevines; he built several
high wooden screens for planting standard and hybrid varieties, and
on a slope below his flower gardens he had a grapery enclosed in
glass. His fruit trees included sixty varieties of pears, for which he
built a drying tower, an apple orchard, cherries, figs, plums, peaches,
apricots, persimmon, paw paw, and the Portuguese quince. He had
a hot house in which he force fed plants and flowers and, near the
house, a formal boxwood garden with arrangements of marigolds,
phlox, roses, peonies, pansies, and hollyhocks. The author of the
line "The groves were God's first temples" was of course also a
great lover of trees.

Bryant was by no means just a weekend amateur horticulturist.
His son-in-law and biographer Parke Godwin reports: "His delight
in his garden was so great it is doubtful whether any shrub or tree

fit for planting in the soil of Long Island, of which he happened to hear, escaped his experiments. If a desireable flower or fruit was mentioned to him, he sent for it, not only to Michigan and California, but to Australia and Japan; and, when he received the precious exotic, he watched over it with the care and attention of a parent over a child."

"The Planting of the Apple-Tree," too often overlooked by anthologists of our day, is one of Bryant's better Roslyn poems. Bryant's characteristic themes emerge organically from his description of the planting of the fruit tree: the inevitability of death, the renewal of life, the continuity between generations and civilizations, and the poet's tenuous role as horticulturist of the spirit. These are themes which also preoccupied Bryant's younger political comrade, literary admirer, and walking companion on the streets of Brooklyn (and possibly even at Cedarmere), Walt Whitman, through many editions of *Leaves of Grass*. If we can tolerate the inversion of Bryant's internally rhymed refrain, we find a richly detailed, finely modulated portrayal of a rural activity which, as in Frost's poems, suggests more than we realize at first.

First we see the preparations for planting the tree, an act of renewal. The imagery, as elemental as Roethke's in "The Greenhouse Sequence," implies that this planting will nurture future generations. With tender care Bryant lays in roots, sifts and presses "the dark mould" around them "As, round the sleeping infant's feet,/We softly fold the cradle-sheet." Beginning several stanzas with the refrain, he envisions nature's bounty that will fall around the maturing tree, follows it through the seasons, and eventually spirals outward from the local rural scene to life in other times and places.

Then, true to form, Bryant anticipates the passing of his generation and confronts his own mortality. As this tree grows bigger and more productive, "we/Shall hear no longer, where we lie,/The summer's songs, the autumn's sigh,/In the boughs of this apple tree." The poem seems headed for a sentimental nineteenth-century conclusion. In the second-last stanza, the imagined wasting away of the tree and the questions about life in the future are about to burgeon into full-scale melodrama when Bryant steps back, takes a hard look at himself, and concludes with a wry, self-mocking portrait:

> "Who planted this old apple-tree?"
> The children of that distant day
> Thus to some aged man shall say;
> And, gazing on its mossy stem,
> The gray-haired man shall answer them:
> "A poet of the land was he,
> Born in the rude but good old times;
> 'Tis said he made some quaint old rhymes
> On planting the apple-tree."

Even the old man quoted within the framework of the poem has apparently not read the poet's "quaint old rhymes." At his worst, Bryant could certainly be quaint and sentimental, but the poet who wrote "The Planting of the Apple-Tree" was too shrewd a prophet for everyone's good. This is a poem that should be read.

In "The Third of November, 1861," his sixty-seventh birthday, Bryant again invites the reader into the circle of his country life in Roslyn. In the second and third stanzas he paints a lush picture of life in the country:

> Tenderly the season has spared the grassy meadows,
>   Spared the petted flowers that the old world gave the new,
> Spared the autumn rose and the garden's group of pansies,
>   Late-blown dandelions and periwinkles blue.
>
> On my cornice linger the ripe black grapes ungathered;
>   Children fill the groves with echoes of their glee,
> Gathering tawny chestnuts, and shouting when beside them
>   Drops the heavy fruit of the tall black walnut tree.

In the midst of all this life, however, the aging Bryant can't help but feel out of place. He is, after all, sixty-seven. Bryant's feelings of mortality dominate the second half of the poem; he interprets the rural scene as allegory of his own life. He asks for such a gentle, graceful conclusion to his life: "Like this kindly season may life's decline come o'er me." He asks that he be warm of heart and cheerful of mind in his last years.

In "Among the Trees" Bryant also uses details of the Roslyn landscape to question his place in the cycle of life. A poem with a broader thematic base than "The Third of November, 1861," it deals with Bryant's relationship to past ages and civilizations as reflected in the forms of life he sees around his country home. The first half of the poem is a survey of the distance between man and nature. As Frost would later do in "The Need of Being Versed in Country Things," Bryant admits that nature is indifferent to the plight of human beings. In the second half, he looks at a famous oak which, as we know from contemporary descriptions, stood between the spring-fed lake (the previous owner, Joseph Moulton, had called the place Springbank) and the bay. This tree conjures up a history Bryant can never know. He does not know who spared this oak when the land that became his property was being cleared. Whoever preserved the oak bequeathed future generations a visible tie between their age and the time when Indians hunted local woods. "An unremembered past," Bryant senses,

> Broods, like a presence, mid the long gray boughs
> Of this old tree, which has outlived so long
>   the fleeting generations of mankind.

Bryant here returns to a theme he had treated in two of his great poems, "Thanatopsis" and "The Prairies."

Toward the end of the poem, Bryant also looks at the famous pear trees under which he gave the annual August feast for Roslyn schoolchildren. He is said to have erected a swing for the children, let them romp over his grounds, and joined in their fun. Searching these fruit trees for clues to the past, he again concedes:

> I ask in vain
> Who planted on the slope this lofty group
> Of ancient pear-trees that with spring-time burst
> Into such breadth of bloom.

He gives thanks to whoever planted the trees, looks to the children's future, and asks for a "nobler age than ours" that will be free from war and fraud.

Bryant confronts the problem of mortality in several other Roslyn poems. In "The Stream of Life" and "The Voice of Autumn," two unsuccessful poems, Bryant gives an impersonal view of the passing of life as reflected by the rural setting. In "The New and the Old," a more personal and moving poem, Bryant confesses that he feels out of place in his country home in the midst of spring. He asks what he is doing "Silver-haired, like a snow-flake thrown/On the greens of the springing year." "The Snow Shower," an effective blending of the personal with the general, is one of the more successful Roslyn poems. It has a sureness of tone, a fullness of detail, and a steady rhythm that drifts outward into the mysteries of life and death evoked by the lake into which he and his companion, apparently his wife but perhaps the reader as well, stare. They watch as "flake after flake" sinks, dissolves, drowns, lies, is lost, or comes to rest "in the dark and silent lake." This steady, inevitable progression suggests the disappearance of family and friends. There is no resolution at the end, just a glimpse into the depths and a rippling sense of mystery.

Bryant may have been able to banish the drudgery of political journalism from Cedarmere, but he was too involved in the issues of his time to use his country home as a retreat from the turmoil of the Civil War. Indeed, ever since he moved from Massachusetts to New York he had been in the thick of political controversy. As Allan Nevins has shown in *The Evening Post: A Century of Political Journalism*, Bryant was strongly anti-tariff from the start, a position that riled his native New England; as early as 1836 he aggressively defended the rights of Abolitionists when other New York City papers were denouncing them; he championed workers' rights to collective bargaining in 1836, when labor unions were being prosecuted as "conspiracies." Before 1840, he was anti-slavery; in 1844 he embarrassed Secretary of State John C. Calhoun by publishing drafts of a treaty which would have brought Texas into the Union as a slave state. (When questioned, Bryant maintained that he did not know how the document ever got to his desk.) In 1860 Bryant introduced Abraham Lincoln to a New York City audience, backed him as the Republican candidate, then influenced him to appoint S. P. Chase to his cabinet; but during the Civil War Bryant repeatedly criticized Lincoln's indecision, the incompetence of his generals, and his delay in emancipating the slaves. One editorial so stung the President that he replied personally.

In two poems set in Roslyn, the Civil War undermines the domestic tranquility and natural harmony of rural life. In "My Autumn Walk," the autumn landscape immediately takes on overtones of death. Bryant sees as "beautiful" the "death-sleep" of those who have fought in the "holy quarrel." He looks around at the Long Island dwellings, crofts, gardens, orchards and knows that messengers of victory will also bring with them bitter news of death. In "The Return of the Birds," the Civil War again disturbs the natural rhythms of rural life. The birds have returned early from the south because of the devastation of war. As if to reassure himself that rural harmony, domestic peace, and natural order will be restored after the war, Bryant imagines the grass turning green and the crocus

"peep[ing]/Beside the housewife's door."

This domestic imagery leads to three concluding Roslyn poems which Bryant wrote about his wife, Frances Fairchild Bryant. In some letters Bryant hints that he was motivated to buy a place in the country because of her chronic poor health. He had written several poems about her before, most notably "O Fairest of the Rural Maids," which Poe singled out for his highest praise. The Roslyn poems show that he not only equated her with the place; for the western-Massachusetts-born poet and statesman who never could feel completely at home in New York City, the woman who grew up in Great Barrington became the very spirit of this special Long Island place. In "The Twenty-seventh of March," her birthday, Bryant flirts with sentimentality from the start. Her birth should have been in June when everything is in bloom. Or that's what a poet would say, he counters, before continuing in what he claims must be "a humbler strain." Perhaps the time of her birth is after all fitting, for then "March . . . begins/To soften into April." Periwinkle, ground laurel, and squirrel cups are then in bloom. Like the modest beauties of nature visible around his Long Island home, his wife's beauty may be "nestled away," but hints of "a world of promise."

Mrs. Bryant died in July of 1866. Several months later Bryant wrote "October, 1866," a poem which according to Parke Godwin formed the conclusion to an unpublished memoir that Bryant wrote about her agonizing last days, her family background, and their life together. This memoir was among the papers which Nassau County received when it was willed Cedarmere in 1976. The poem appeared in Parke Godwin's edition of Bryant's works, but the memoir has never been published, perhaps because of the stricture in the first paragraph:

> What I write here is intended for my own eyes and those of my children. For my own eye, lest if I should live much longer, some of the minuter particulars, so interesting to myself may fade from a memory which I cannot but expect will be weakened by old age. For the eyes of my children that it may revive in their minds a memory pleasant, though sad, of one who was most dear to them and who was, in all respects an example of goodness such as is rarely seen.

In the next paragraph, Bryant describes the simple ceremony conducted the day before in the cemetery he had recently helped to establish:

> Fanny Fairchild Bryant, my beloved wife and my loving companion for forty-five years and more, is dead. We buried her yesterday in the new cemetery at this place, on the edge of the woodland which had lately been pierced — with roads and walks — in the first grave dug in my little enclosure there. The funeral was private — a few friends being asked, principally from town, to be present.

Some remarks near the end of the memoir about the role she played in Bryant's life as a writer demonstrate that the piece is of importance to more than family:

> For my part all my plans had some reference either to her approbation or her pleasure. I never wrote a poem that I did not repeat it to her and her judgment upon it. I found its success with the public was in proportion to the impression it made upon her. She loved my verses and judged them kindly but liked not all my poems equally. In her last illness I

recited to her the last poem I had written, "The Death of Slavery." She listened and then said, "My illness unfits me to judge of it as well as if I were in health," and then added a word or two of kind appreciation. There is nobody now to whose friendly but always sincere and discriminating judgment I can look to perform the same office.

In "October, 1866" Bryant revisits Frances' grave in the local cemetery landscaped to look like a rural park. Especially in the spring, when the dogwood, azalea, and lilac are in full bloom around the family plot where Bryant was buried next to his wife just over a hundred years ago, Roslyn Cemetery still evokes the feelings of serenity and harmony that the most distinguished citizen of his age enjoyed here. In this poem Bryant brings flowers to his wife's grave, looks out over the Long Island landscape, and recalls with considerable pain the life they had shared in Roslyn. A birch tree "drops its bright spoil like arrowheads of gold" as "Sailspotted, blue and lake-like sleeps the sound." In the context of the setting, the new cemetery, and the recent death of his wife, this is a deeply suggestive line which rolls with a beautifully pensive music. Bryant cannot enjoy the scene any longer; as he had insisted nine years before in the poem to his daughter, he could not fully enjoy the charms of Roslyn by himself. As if to console himself, he concludes that the spirit of this beloved woman has come to rest in this place they have both loved.

"May Evening" dramatizes the painful associations brought about by spring in Roslyn now that his wife is dead. Spring breezes enter the rooms that have become "silent" in her absence. In Bryant's mind, the rebirth in nature is transformed into death: the breath of nature passes over sassafras blossoms and the spice bush but comes away "embalmed." The grieving husband tries to take consolation in his knowledge that there are nearby cottages in which the peace and joy he has known in Roslyn still flourish. In the last line he looks out from within his personal darkness for "the return of [the] day" which he had often seen dawn in Roslyn.

Even more so than his poems, Bryant's letters pulse with affection for his "half country life" in Roslyn. Such poems as "The Planting of the Apple-Tree," "The Snow Shower," "The Tides," and "The Rain Dream," however, show that Roslyn did indeed move Bryant to write good poetry. If these particular poems do not ascend to the heights or plumb the depths he reached in "Thanatopsis," "To a Waterfowl," "The Prairies," or the sonnet to his painter friend Cole, they are nonetheless poems we must read if we are to recover a part of the heritage we have been too patronizing to appreciate. To borrow a phrase from "The Poet," a compelling poetic flight which does not take off from any particular landscape, in the Roslyn poems "the warm current tingles." If Bryant's words do not always seem to "burn" in these poems, at least they glow.

VINCE CLEMENTE

Bryant's "To a Waterfowl" and the Painter W. S. Mount

ALTHOUGH WILLIAM CULLEN BRYANT and William Sidney Mount often met in the 1840s and 1850s in private homes during meetings of the Sketch Club, as the Club's minutes establish, and although they had mutual friends like the painters Thomas Cole and Asher Durand, no record of their conversation is extant. Since the poet's Cedarmere at Roslyn was just thirty-five miles west of the painter's family home at Stony Brook, however, they were practically neighbors, and I can imagine their conversation.

I picture them along the pedestrian walk-deck of the steamer that made its bi-weekly run from Stony Brook to New York, stopping at Hempstead Harbor for the commuter William Cullen Bryant en route to his New York *Evening Post* offices. I can hear their talk: Mount's meeting with Washington Irving at the Tarrytown home; their treks to the Thomas Cole studio in the Catskill Mountains; Cole's sudden death in 1848. The older man must have listened patiently as the younger lamented Walt Whitman's piece, "Something about Art and Brooklyn Artists" in the February 1, 1851 edition of the *Evening Post,* a review that reduced the black subject of Mount's *The Lucky Throw* to so much "Ethiopian minstrelsy." I can see Bryant's apologetic demeanor.

Although this scenario is all conjecture, there are many actual "connections." One such is a letter from Mount to Bryant, dated May 6, 1857: the painter-inventor informs the poet-editor of a recently completed design, with illustrations included, for a paddle-driven steamboat that "can be driven from New York to Albany in one hundred eighty minutes." Mount ends his letter, "You may let the public know of this plan, if you think proper," indicative of his faith in the editor's judgment. The postscript is as revealing: "I regret to hear of Crawford's illness." He had in mind their mutual friend Thomas Crawford, whose *Armed Freedom* mounts the dome of the Capitol in Washington and who died later that year. Although the letter's salutation begins with the formal, "My Dear Sir," one gleans from the general tone that the content is the result of prior conversation.

There is also extant a letter-fragment dated 1861, intended for The National Academy of Design. Mount writes: "The National Academy of Design contains some of the greatest names . . . that the country has produced . . . our poets William Cullen Bryant, Fitz Green Halleck, and Washington Irving." He did indeed see Bryant as a tower of a man, and one can imagine his pleasure when earlier the European art firm of Goupil, Vibert and Company proposed a series of portraits of outstanding Americans to be called "American Portrait Gallery." The series, to include twelve such portraits, began with Daniel Webster, William Cullen Bryant, and William Sidney Mount. Mount the country bumpkin was certainly in august company.

Although Mount is best known as the 19th century's finest genre painter, the Long Islander who chronicled the local, the every day, the stuff of his village life – spearing for eels and flat fish, corn-husking, drawing water, hay-making – like his New England counterparts he was an inveterate diarist, writing almost daily entries. The real Bryant–Mount jointure is to be found in the journals: Mount's four references to Bryant's "To a Waterfowl," beginning with an April 18, 1847 entry and concluding with a December, 1858 notation. Painting "To a Waterfowl" became for him a moral imperative, one may even say an obsession, as he recorded in 1858: "Bryant's Water Fowl – I must make a study."

The "Water Fowl" citations are not isolated eruptions but rather part of the psychic fabric of the journal's tissue, the journal graph of Mount's inner landscape. These notations appear as either an item in a list of "Subjects" to be completed or as exhortations to the tired, wavering self. They also set in motion a series of related images, an "association of ideas," much the way Bryant pieced together "To a Waterfowl," building upon the initial sensory perception of the solitary water bird.

The first reference is found in a journal entry of April 18, 1847: "We must dare to do what we see, which requires some moral courage." And then, as if summoning up this "moral courage," he sets down an exhausting list of "Subjects" to paint. Even at a cursory glance, one recognizes a common theme, isolation, each subject traveling its "solitary way," each like Mount, a detached isolato, and like the fowl "tread[ing] alone."

He begins his catalogue with a lone "figure sitting at the root of a tree reading or meditating." His mind moves to " 'Woodman spare that tree.' The water fowl. Morris and Bryant." And by association, he darts to a series of castaways: "Babes in the woods, or the lost ones. The lost Boy, or the runaway. A man carrying a bag of grain on his shoulder." It isn't farfetched to interpret these "figures" as

objectifications of Mount's central life conflict, the self-imposed iso-
lation of his artist's calling at odds with his deep-welling social
nature, his huge-hearted communal self.

I'd like to suggest a Bryant parallel, that the image of the effulgent
bird was also for the poet objectification of a gnawing ambivalence.
As William Cullen Bryant II writes in "The Waterfowl in Retro-
spect," in the June, 1957 issue of *The New England Quarterly*, "The
truth is that young Bryant had for several years been terrified by the
thought of having to speak publicly in court. Judge Samuel Howe
[his legal mentor at Worthington, near Cummington] had feared
that the boy's shyness would handicap him in arguing legal cases."
In fact, just months before his admission to the Massachusetts bar,
Bryant had confessed to a friend, "The nearer I approach to it the
more I dread it."

In July 1815, while he was a clerk in the office of Congressman
William Baylies at Bridgewater, near Plymouth in eastern Massa-
chusetts, one evening his imagination seized upon a lone bird,
"darkly seen against the crimson sky." And the young man of
twenty, suddenly come of age, unable to postpone any longer
making a living, found in the waterfowl a kindred spirit: vulnerable
to the fowler "to do thee wrong" as he would be exposed "in a hall
of justice" to "hoary-headed wranglers," as he wrote in 1875, in the
retrospective poem "A Lifetime."

The second journal notation was recorded three years later, on
April 25, 1850, the year he completed a preliminary sketch for
George P. Morris' poem "Woodman, Spare That Tree" & about
the time he attended the National Academy of Design exhibit,
which included Asher Durand's rendering of Bryant's "Thanatop-
sis." The entry is little more than a list of projected projects:" . . . a
picture for James Lenox . . . a picture for Mr. J. Sturges. Also,
Woodman Spare that Tree, for G. P. Morris and one from Bryant's

Water Fowl." He concludes with, "I must paint every day if pos-
sible." "I must" are operative words, and we shall see how in the
next citation Mount shifts the imperative "must" to Bryant.

Ten months later, on February 12, 1851, he writes: " 'Woodman
spare that tree,' next if possible," and continues the self-castigation
with, "Perseverance will overcome difficulties." He then veers to
a common theme that declares his ambivalence, "I should paint
more if I didn't live in Stony Brook . . . be more among strangers . . .
new scenery and strange characters will compel me to paint." He
concludes with the Bryant behest: "I must paint one picture from
Bryant's poetry." We see here how central to his psychic health the
subject is.

The final reference, merely dated "1858," is an item in a list of
"Subjects," but the subjects well from a common emotional plexis.
They are forlorn castaways – isolatos. Mount notes: "A white man
looking at the grave of Uncle Tom, Bryant's water fowl – I must
make a study. Woodman spare that tree. For G. P. Morris. . . . A
child playing with a sun beam, an old man standing at the grave of
his mother." He ends with lines from an unnamed poem by an
obscure nineteenth-century poet, Lewis Hess, lines in imagery and
theme remarkably close to the Bryant poem. It is as if Mount,
through indirection, were preparing preliminary sketches for a paint-
ing he would never undertake, the Hess lines unlocking the long-
submerged Bryant voice. But first, a look at the subjects.

They are part of the journal tissue that is Mount's psychic graph,
but each is as well a striking image, a genre miniature canvas, very
much like the pictorial technique at work in Bryant's autobiograph-
ical poem, "A Lifetime," where each stanza is a tableau culled from
the poet's long life.

In the summer of 1875, visiting his Cummington home for one
last look, he felt, as he had never before, memories of his boyhood

course through him. The poem that followed shaped itself as a series of "pictures in an exhibition," and if there is a common theme, it is one of the child unattended entering the natural mysteries. We see this in stanza-pictures: "A delicate child and slender,/With lock of light-brown hair,/From knoll to knoll is leaping/In the breezy summer air," and "I look again, and there rises/A forest wide and wild,/And in it the boy is wandering,/No longer a little child." We are then privy to the poet's genesis as "He murmurs his own rude verses/As he roams the woods alone;/And again I gaze with wonder,/His eyes are so like my own." Finally, Bryant plucks from time the young poet in his self-imposed isolation: "I see him in his chamber,/Where he sits him down to write/The rhymes he framed in his ramble,/And he cons them with delight." The rhythms for his poems he first heard during these woodland "rambles," just as Mount abstracted from his native Stony Brook sandstone the pigments for his paintings.

The final "Waterfowl" reference is significant as well for the Hess lines, so close to Bryant's in rhythm and imagery that one would expect Mount to get to the painting at once. He wrote in his journal: " 'At dawn . . ./When the first lark shall plume his wing, and soar from bondage free,/To warble forth some merry notes,/Then give one thought to me./ . . . And when the shades of evening are fast falling into night,/An hour, that well seems made for thought, and quiet is in delight. . . ." But Mount stopped there, never to find his "subject" again.

But he did, in 1850, complete a preliminary study after Morris' "Woodman, Spare That Tree." This study, oil on paper, is lost but survives as a photograph. Bryant thought enough of the poem to include it in his 1870 *Library of Poetry and Song*, in the section called "Poems of Childhood." The study is a typical Mount genre depiction: a cottage recessed in a deep wood, the dutiful wife resting on a porch, her eyes riveted on her husband, the "woodsman" about to fell a large oak that dominates the canvas, and in the lower right corner, a venerable figure in ministerial black, left arm raised in entreaty, pleading, "Woodsman, spare that tree." Mount was surely drawn to the Morris poem for the very reasons he was drawn to the Bryant poem — its "Long Island" imagery and its moralizing tone, qualities I'll elaborate on later.

Although the Morris poem, which was also a favorite of Poe's, reads like doggerel, lines such as the following must have stabbed Mount's heart, as it must have Bryant's: "My mother kissed me here;/My father pressed my hand —/Forgive this foolish tear,/But let that old oak stand!"

However, there are deeper connections that explain why in the journal the poems appear in tandem. Both the woodsman, bent on downing an ancient oak, and the fowler, prepared to "mark thy distant flight to do thee wrong," are interlopers, violators of the natural order, intruders in a world Mount saw as a "cradle of harmony."

As Mount corresponded with Bryant, so too did he correspond with George P. Morris, editor of the prominent *New York Mirror* from 1823 to 1842, the publication that covered the American art scene, reporting the "current happenings in the art world," reviewing local exhibitions, and reproducing the paintings of Cole, Durand, & Mount. One would think that the preliminary sketch of "Woodsman" would only prod Mount to begin to sketch out details for "Water Fowl."

Why he never undertook the project, we'll never know; we do understand, however, the appeal, the lure of Bryant's poem. In the bird, Mount found a kindred spirit, another "isolato," who at day's end continues its "solitary way." I imagine his heart racing, reading the poem for the first time, finding in the waterfowl objectification of his own estrangement, his own ambulatory life. Those final

months before his sudden death in the fall of 1868, he was a boarder
— either with family or friends or with local farmers. Never a man
of property, he wrote again and again in his journals, "Better to
wear out than to rust out in one place."

One feels the hurt of his alienation in lines like the following:
"In this retired region where I have no artist to converse with . . .
the loneliness and stillness here is getting to be quite painful for
me" (December 3, 1847 letter). "I believe a true painter should have
no home — but to wander in search of scenery and character during
spring, summer, autumn. . . . Better be moving than rusting out
in one place" (November 17, 1852 journal). And finally, the voice
admonishes the trapped self: "Must you confine yourself to Stony
Brook forever?" (March 19, 1854 journal)

Even into his final years, Mount was a man who lived on the run,
designing both a portable studio, first such in the Republic, and a
skiff, the *Pond Lily*, from which to paint. There was something of
the gypsy in his makeup, this Long Islander on his "solitary way."
I can imagine his saying over and over, from the portable studio,
Bryant's lines: "All day thy wings have fanned/At that far height,
the cold, thin atmosphere,/Yet stoop not weary, to the welcome
land,/Though the dark night is near."

"To a Waterfowl" also preoccupied Mount because it articulated
for him, as only poetry can, a lifetime tension, one never to be
resolved. This isolato, this transient-boarder needed, even enjoyed,
the company of people. The end of the bird's wandering is com-
munion: "And soon that toil shall end;/Soon shalt thou find a sum-
mer home, and rest,/And scream among thy fellows; reeds shall
bend,/Soon o'er thy sheltered nest." The bird will finally "rest,"
find repose, but only "among thy fellows." Savoring camaraderie,
Mount did "scream among his fellows," while guarding his private,
artist-self.

The man who wrote only months before his death, in a rented farmhouse room, "It is better to board among strangers," is the man who nonetheless walked the eight miles from Stony Brook to Smithtown to play "the fife for the Stony Brook and Smithtown Fusiliers." His fellow townspeople remembered him as a man who had freely given himself to "that paradise of loafers, amusing himself and his friends with his fiddle and pencil sketches." Little wonder then that Mount's best pictures, *Eel Spearing, Farmers Nooning, Dance of the Haymakers*, depict communal life, a life he both desired and feared.

As he responded to the poem's depiction of his lifetime tension, so he responded to its moralizing strain. How well he must have understood Bryant's leap to faith: "There is a Power whose care/ Teaches thy way along the pathless coast —/The desert and illimitable air." Bryant's benevolent God spoke to Mount's spiritual core. In 1866, looking back over his artist's life, he remembered how "When I commenced art in 1825 . . . I asked God in my humble way to strengthen my love for art, and in His goodness, He directed me to a closer observation of nature. And I gained strength in art." In all corners of his Setauket–Stony Brook world, he saw the hand of his Godhead, "directing me to closer observations of nature." He encountered, firsthand, Bryant's "Power whose care/Teaches. . . ."

Little wonder, then, that he called the violin he designed and patented his "cradle of harmony." Harmony was a lived experience for Mount. He was never without his tuning fork, carrying it in his pantaloon hip pocket along with his journal. This tuning fork was more than musical implement; it became a governing archetypal symbol. Striking the fork, he sounded the world's "primal sanities," its benevolence.

The moralizing note in "To a Waterfowl" must have enchanted Mount, and nowhere is this moral vein as deep as in the final stanza:

"He, who from zone to zone,/Guides through the boundless sky thy certain flight,/In the long way that I must tread alone,/Will lead my steps aright." I'm sure Mount carried such certainty with him to the grave, as did his beloved brother, the painter Shepard A-lonzo Mount, who died two months to the day before Mount. The brother's final words, as Mount was to report, were, as he looked "with admiration into the spirit world, 'How beautiful. . . . I am coming.' " Mount's final words went with him to the "spirit world"; however, I imagine his saying something like the final lines in Bryant's "To a Fringed Gentian": "Hope, blossoming within my heart,/May look to heaven as I depart."

A painter, Mount *saw* "To a Waterfowl" as well as heard its controlled line. Its pictorial quality must have had enormous appeal to him. "While glow the heavens with the last steps of day" may have suggested the crimson wing-bar of dusk above Crane Neck, while at long day's end, from his portable studio, he sketched a brilliant sunset. And the poem, out of coastal eastern Massachusetts, in its imagery suggests Mount's coastal Long Island home:

> Seek'st thou the plashy brink
> Of weedy lake, or marge of river wide,
> Or where the rocking billows rise and sink
> On the chafed ocean-side?

"Plashy brink," "weedy lake," "river wide," "rocking billows," and "chafed ocean-side" are not only the liquid images in Mount's paintings and sketches but also the primordial images out of his boyhood — his own amniotic fluids — his "playfields": the Sound below Crane Neck; Conscience Bay; the Harbors at Stony Brook and Setauket; the Mill Pond, where as a boy he fished for perch.

The waterfowl's trek ends as it finds "a summer home," where "reeds . . . bend,/. . . o'er thy sheltered nest." How often had Mount witnessed such a quintessential Long Island tableau, staring into the shore reeds along Stony Brook Harbor, a lone Canada goose nesting in the spartina, the autumn hassocks cornhusk yellow.

Mount's transcription of "To a Waterfowl" would have been the ideal realization of the union of painting and poetry, the one enriching the other, and I can envision the completed project. Mount, who was not unwilling to learn from other painters, would have borrowed from his friend Asher Durand. Durand's 1850 rendering of Bryant's "Thanatopsis" would serve as inspiration, as touchstone for the "Waterfowl" painting.

Mount wrote in his journal for April 18, 1850, under the heading, "Exhibitions, 1850": "Landscape composition from Bryant's Thanatopsis. . . . Durand says objects in shadows should be more or less flat to make distance. . . . A picture should have repose." *Repose* is the operative word. No doubt he also had in mind the serenity and "repose" of Durand's *Kindred Spirits*, completed in 1849, a year after Cole's sudden death. The painting places Cole and his dear friend Bryant precariously on a cliff, jutting into an unspoiled, pristine world in which they are indeed "kindred spirits."

Had Mount painted "To a Waterfowl," he would have aimed for this repose, this equipoise. The painting would have been for him a summation, an attempt to resolve the paradox that had stalked him for a lifetime: the ambulatory, village boarder needed desperately a "summer home, and rest," his own "sheltered nest." In his most autobiographical work, Mount himself, perhaps, would hope to find a place for the heart to rest. I imagine a local setting, possibly the spartina meadow along Stony Brook Harbor, and the waterfowl, perhaps a ghostly little blue heron he sighted again and again during his village sauntering. It is such a shy bird, and so like the soul in flight.

I'd also like to envision Mount's technique. He would have employed a style he had used just once before, in *Crane Neck Across the Marsh*, his only painting that is both undated and unsigned, as if he wished anonymity for such a work. "To a Waterfowl" would also have been a break with the genre spirit, and a projection of Mount's inner vision upon his objective phenomenal world.

Crane Neck Across the Marsh has been called by critics a precursor of the avant-garde, Mount's 100-year leap ahead to abstract expressionism. Lacking incident and pigmentation, with an almost uniform brownish tonality, the painting projects an unrelieved horizon above a marshland that slowly moves to an eerie Crane Neck, jutting through what appears to be rising morning mist. The viewer's eye then rests on three figures as imperceptible as an ant colony, lost in the immensity of a brooding, indifferent natural world, out-of-place interlopers. The painting itself, in its totality of impact, suggests Bryant's "pathless coast −/. . . desert and illimitable air," the abyss that could swallow the bird were it not for the "Power whose care/Teaches thy way. . . ." This "Power" is absent in *Crane Neck*.

Crane Neck is Mount's darkest moment, his giving in to despair, the dark night of the soul when he felt connected to nothing, his once-familiar Setauket–Stony Brook fields become a "pathless coast." "To a Waterfowl" would have been his affirmation, a work like Melville's *Billy Budd*, an attempt in old age to resolve the antinomies. Before this final and hard-won victory, however, Mount must first pass through old and feared ground and take the risks he did in *Crane Neck*. But there would have been victory. The lone little blue heron I imagine in the spartina hassock along Stony Brook Harbor would signify, in its pure serenity and equipoise, the God-struggle of both Bryant and Mount — their "lone wandering" but final victory.

RICHARD WILBUR

A Word from Cummington

THERE ARE IN CUMMINGTON (population 600-odd) a few histori-
cally-minded people who know of that Bryant who, during his half-
century of journalism in New York, was a militant advocate of the
right to strike, a strong voice against slavery, a furtherer of the arts,
a force behind the planning of Central Park, and the proprietor of a
semi-rural retreat in Roslyn. But for the most part in Cummington
we think of him (somewhat vaguely) as America's first eminent
poet, and as an admirable man who, first and last, had much to do
with the town. There is a marker on the site of his birthplace, near
the Dawes Cemetery. The house in which he grew up, and which
in his latter years he purchased and enlarged for summer use –
raising the structure on jacks and constructing a new first floor be-
neath it – is now a cultural landmark administered by the Trustees
of Reservations. Downhill from the Homestead is a ravine which
was never cleared, as the better part of Cummington was in his
boyhood, because it was too rugged and steep to be useful; its acres
of giant timber, still standing, must have predisposed the young
Bryant to become a poet of "wild nature" and an enthusiast of
natural sublimities in painting. I hear that a newly-made path gives
access to the area, and I am glad of the fact, because I have never
beaten my way into that forest without being much bloodied by
brambles; it would please Bryant, too, who wrote some of his best
lines on the subject of path-making. Cummington is grateful for the
stone library which Bryant gave to the town in 1872, for the several
thousand books with which he stocked it, and for the librarian's

house which he built nearby; he also gave the land, and much of the money, for a long-used Bryant Schoolhouse.

He is our great man, and one or more of his poems is likely to be read aloud on any of our ceremonial occasions. Yet I suppose that as a personality he somewhat escapes our imaginations. To be sure, the visitor to the Homestead may come near him by responding to his delicate drawings of the local flora; and the chinning-bar in the closet of his bedroom, over which the aged man repeatedly hoisted his beard each morning, may recall his reputation as a vigorous person and a strenuous hiker. What estranges him from us is the tone of many of his poems — sonorous, grave, noble, edifying, oratorically ruminative. What we miss in him, a fair bit of the time, is what we find (to make an outrageous contrast) in John Donne. In Donne, we hear a complex man talking, whereas Bryant sometimes sounds like a statue. Concentrating on a fluent orotundity, Bryant's poems too often lack the spontaneous figure, the surprisingly accurate word. Nor does one feel, as often as one would like to, that the world of which he speaks offers much resistance to the flow of his speech — that it has a life of its own. In "Inscription for the Entrance to a Wood," we meet "the squirrel, with raised paws erect," and cannot believe that he will ever move: he is a generic and illustrative squirrel, a step in a melodious argument and not a critter. Later, the "trunks of prostrate trees," because the poet is contending that unfallen Nature is glad, are obliged to "breathe fixed tranquillity." I am prepared to be persuaded of the goodness of all Nature, or of all things, but I would like to see some struggle toward that conclusion, some admission of contrary evidence, as in Whitman's "Song of Myself." Bryant's poem simply imposes the notion on its data — though it must be granted that the beautiful closing lines about the wind, because they allow the wind some initiative and because its behavior is plausible, go far toward saving the day.

"Thanatopsis," which my father took pleasure in declaiming over the shaving-bowl, is another poem in which elevation of style masks from the reader and from the poet the insufficiency of its argument. Underlying the poem, undoubtedly, is a Deistic persuasion that God made Nature, and that all things natural, including death, must therefore be all right. But the poem does not coherently say that. It tells us, rather gloomily, that in death we shall be reduced to the elements, losing our "individual being." It then gives us some sort of counter-movement, wherein it is said that in death one has the company of the great of the past, and indeed of the whole of the dead, Earth being "the great tomb of man." This magnification of one's dust neither fortifies nor consoles; number and space and duration and "majesty" are simply laid on as a rhetorical enhancement. The closing section then confuses matters by describing physical dissolution, which is not mysterious, as an entry into a "mysterious realm," and urges an "unfaltering trust" in something unspecified. The effect of this is to give an air of bad faith or two-mindedness to the poem's Biblical echoes and its suggestions of individual persistence ("sleep," "rest," "pleasant dreams.")

I have put off some of my Cummington friends by doubting the merits of "Thanatopsis," but fortunately it is possible to be two-minded about Bryant, who did after all write some truly superior poems. The yellow violet, which I had never seen before moving to the Berkshires, is strewn along all of our timber-trails in spring, and it seems to me that Bryant's well-known poem of that title does the flower double justice. In the first place, the yellow violet is exactly and gracefully described as to the shape and coloration of its blossom, the attitude of the blossom upon the stem, its fragrance, its time of emergence, its association with "the last year's leaves" or "the snow-bank's edges cold." At the same time, without any slighting of the object or any air of exploitation, the plant is made symbolic in two ways at once: such words as "Modest," "peeps," "faint" and "Virgin" work toward one effect, while the ideas of hardiness and sun-brightness in stanzas 3–4 produce another. The result is an emblem of modest excellence so artfully arrived at that a comparatively unforced transition to one of "Nature's teachings" may be made in the seventh stanza.

To speak of yet another famous poem, "To a Waterfowl" strikes me as moving from description to moral with complete success. It is a poem which opens with a question — which inquires as well as asserts or teaches. One of its strengths is that it implicitly admits the possibility of lostness and unbelief and wearily giving up; it proceeds from rosy light to darkness, from the known to the unknown; there are sinister overtones in such words as "solitary," "desert," and "abyss." All of this keeps the poem honest and strengthens its affirmation. The bird and its progress are realized in a fresh, simple, economical language which Bryant tends to lose when he expatiates in enjambed pentameters. There is a fine concreteness in such words as "chafed" and "fanned," a plain eloquence in "Lone wandering, but not lost," and the word "scream" (line 23) brilliantly crowns a description in which the waterfowl is not an illustration but a living fact. There are many more things to praise here, but I shall mention just one: the way that deep calls to deep in this poem, as the "rosy depths" of line 3 are echoed in the "deeply" of line 27, thus further weaving the moral into the experience. I suppose, if there must be rankings and priorities, that "To a Waterfowl" may be America's first flawless poem.

WILLIAM JAY SMITH

The Bryant Cottage in Cummington

I HAD COME to spend the weekend with my old friends poet Richard
Wilbur and his wife Charlee before flying off to France for the
summer of 1966. The Wilburs had just bought a house in Cumming-
ton, Massachusetts, and their enthusiasm for the area was boundless.
I had also known Cummington briefly years before when I had come
over several times from Pownal, Vermont, to visit Harry Duncan
and Paul Williams, who ran the Cummington Press. Paul Williams
had died and Harry Duncan had long since departed for Iowa, taking
the press with him. The town of Cummington, still a rural commu-
nity midway between Pittsfield and Northampton, had changed little
over the years. The Wilburs, eager to interest their writer friends in
settling there, suggested that we take a tour of the houses of the
area, of which several beautiful ones were available at what seemed
bargain prices; I might find one to my liking.

"I'm not in the market for a house," I protested.

But they were insistent, and the tour seemed a lark. Guided by
the real-estate agent who had found their house, we went off over
the hills. It was a glorious summer day and we saw some glorious
houses. I remember one in particular on a summit overlooking fields
and orchards in every direction. I could see myself retiring to this
spacious, tastefully remodeled eighteenth-century farmhouse, in-
stalling myself in a book-lined study there and puttering about in
its sweet-smelling fields. But to do so I would have needed an income
four or five times what I then had. Other farms offered similar vistas
and similar lovely, if remote, possibilities. We had spent most of the
afternoon and had seen a good portion of the countryside. I felt

renewed by the spirit of the New England that I had grown to love
as a twenty-five-year resident of Vermont. We were ready to start
home when the agent said that she had just one more place she
wanted to show us — a little mountain retreat. The elderly owner,
who lived in Princeton, scarcely came to Cummington any longer.
He was eager to sell his little house and I could probably have it for
a song.

A retreat indeed it was, I thought, as we wound our way up the
narrow mountain road in Cummington, a few miles from the Wil-
liam Cullen Bryant Homestead. The road was now no more than a
broad path, its center a mound of tufted grass and flowers brushing
against our wheels. The house, a little less than a mile from the
paved road below, was small and well-proportioned. Its gambrel
roof, outlined against tall birches, and luxuriant pale green ferns
enclosing its white clapboards and the bright Indian paint-brush
blooming in its fields gave it a dreamlike, fairy-tale quality. The
house was in good repair but tightly boarded up. When we lifted
the heavy shutters, we found that it consisted of two good-sized
rooms, one on each side of a well-built fireplace, a little entrance-way
with a minute stairway winding up around the chimney to the attic.
There was a small, modestly equipped kitchen, an adjoining bath,
and a narrow porch on the back, enclosed by windows that hooked
up to the ceiling. The real-estate agent knew nothing of the history
of the place but as we made our way around it, light sifting in to
touch the dark walls, Dick Wilbur and I both remarked that some-
thing about the spirit of the place, not just the abundant bookshelves,
suggested strongly that this had once been a writer's dwelling. The
house stood on a wedge-shaped plot of some thirty acres stretching
down to the Westfield River. On the other side of the road were
another two hundred acres that I could probably also purchase. As
we made our way down the hill, the tall grass stroking the sides of

the car, I decided that this little retreat had to be mine. I made an offer and it was immediately accepted.

I had spent the previous week, as I had for many summers, on the staff of the Suffield (Connecticut) Writer–Reader Conference, where I conducted the Poetry Workshop in the company of Louis Untermeyer and Padraic Colum. Since I was to fly from Hartford, I went back to spend the night in Suffield, and I told my friends there of my new acquisition. When I described the house in detail, Padraic Colum came forth with a startling declaration:

"I know the house very well. I wrote *The King of Ireland's Son* there one summer."

Padraic then told me all that he remembered; other parts of the house's history I learned later. The original structure — the two main rooms — had been a wing of the William Cullen Bryant Homestead and had served as Dr. Peter Bryant's medical offices. When the house was sold out of the family in the middle of the last century, the new owners decided that they had no further need of this particular section. They cut it off and sold it to the only black couple in Cummington, who had worked at the Homestead. It was moved around 1842, as houses frequently were at the time, down the hill from the Homestead into another section of Cummington known as Lightning Bug, so-called presumably because of the abundance of fireflies there. I have a photograph of the house as it then stood, looking somewhat battered, its unpainted clapboards askew like ruffled feathers.

In 1914 Mrs. William Vaughn Moody, the wife of the Chicago poet, searching for a New England summer base for her husband, heard that the house had once belonged to William Cullen Bryant and that within its walls he had written his famous poem "Thanatopsis." Christening it then and there "Thanatopsis House," she had it dismantled and moved to where it now stands on farmland she had purchased beside what had once been the main road between Northampton and Pittsfield. She restored it, building a new fireplace and a new stone foundation, and to it added the kitchen, bathroom and porch. Up the hill, toward the Homestead, on the other side of the road, she constructed a large log-cabin, and around these two structures she organized a writers' colony in the twenties and thirties. In the log-cabin the poets would gather for discussion, and there were poetry readings long before such readings became popular on the national scene. The house was occupied during the summer by a number of writers, among them the young Glenway Wescott, also from Chicago, who wrote one of his early novels here. She offered it permanently to Robert Frost, but he declined because there was no high school nearby for his children. Among the other poets who came were Edwin Arlington Robinson, John Masefield, the English Poet Laureate, and the Indian Nobel Prize Winner

Rabindrinath Tagore. Harriet Moody, after her husband's death, had opened a successful catering business in Chicago. She provided her Cummington writing residents with good meals. Supplies came up from town each morning by ox-cart, which took the trash back down. Next to the Bryant Cottage stood the original farmhouse, occupied by Luther Shaw and his wife. Mrs. Shaw helped feed the summer residents; Padraic Colum remembered her excellent pies. The Luther Shaw farmhouse burned down in 1940; our road now bears his name.

As I sat in the plane on the way to Paris after buying this historic house, I wondered if I had taken leave of my senses. Why did I need a house in the first place, and if so, did I need one with so many literary ghosts? I was planning to marry a French woman who had never lived in America. What was she going to think of a husband who on the spur of the moment had invested most of his capital in a house that could clearly not be occupied the year round and could at best serve only as a country retreat? I married Sonja in September and when she arrived to join me a month and a half later at Williams College, where I was then Poet-in-Residence, I took her over to see the Bryant Cottage, as I had decided to call it. (I refused from the beginning to adopt Mrs. Moody's designation of "Thanatopsis House," since there was no clear evidence that Bryant had written "Thanatopsis" in these rooms and because it seemed too lugubrious a name for so cheerful a residence.) My concern about Sonja's reaction to the house was immediately dispelled as soon as she saw it.

"It's a little jewel," she said.

We discovered in no time how flawed a jewel it was: there was much work to be done, most of it by her, to make it livable. Sonja has a passionate interest in the eighteenth century, and the rooms were ultimately, in every careful detail of color, fabric, and furnish-

ing, to reflect her exquisite taste. But first there were many basic
changes to be made. The kitchen facilities were minimal: the sink
slanted at such an angle that it was impossible to wash a dish with-
out half the soapy water ending up in one's lap. The previous owner,
a physicist, apparently thought that he could repair everything him-
self without calling in anyone to help. The wiring was such a dan-
gerous patchwork that it was a wonder the house had not burned to
the ground years before. The physicist had a mania for hooks: hooks
of every size had been screwed into the walls for what purpose we
could never be sure. It took years to divest the house of all of them.
Of the few pieces of furniture that remained the most important
were two large trestle oak tables that had been made on the place.
One of them became our dining room table and the other my desk,
and so they have remained to this day. We had the house rewired
and installed electric heat and storm windows.

That first winter our road was not plowed, but we kept the heat
on, and once before a heavy snowstorm we were taken up to the
cottage by one of the Cummington residents in his snowmobile. It
was a strange feeling to be deposited there, completely isolated from
the world, in that great white expanse. That weekend I wrote the
following poem, which later appeared in the *New Yorker*:

WINTER MORNING

>All night the wind swept over the house
>And through our dream,
>Swirling the snow up through the pines,
>Ruffling the white, ice-capped clapboards,
>Rattling the windows,
>Rustling around and below our bed
>So that we rode
>Over wild water
>In a white ship breasting the waves.
>We rode through the night

On green, marbled
Water, and, half-waking, watched
The white, eroded peaks of icebergs
Sail past our windows;
Rode out the night in that north country,
And awoke, the house buried in snow,
Perched on a
Chill promontory, a
Giant's tooth
In the mouth of the cold valley,
Its white tongue looped frozen around us,
The trunks of tall birches
Revealing the rib cage of a whale
Stranded by a still stream;
And saw, through the motionless baleen of their branches,
As if through time,
Light that shone
On a landscape of ivory,
A harbor of bone.*

I left Williams the following year to join the faculty of Hollins
College in Virginia, but wherever we have been during the past
eighteen years, in Virginia, in Washington, or New York, we have
returned to spend part of each year in the Bryant Cottage. My step-
son, who came to this country from France at the age of thirteen, has
always thought of it as home. After attending the Boston University
Drama School, he retired to Cummington with his young wife, built
himself a log house halfway up our hill, and proceeded to build and
remodel houses throughout the area. Among his most recent remod-
eling jobs has been a handsome addition to the Bryant Cottage: he
ripped off our sagging back porch and gave us a large living room
with a cathedral ceiling and ample bookshelves with a guestroom

---

* From *The Traveler's Tree: New and Selected Poems* by William Jay Smith,
Persea Books, 1980, copyright © 1980 by William Jay Smith.

and bath below it, and, in the process, extended my study in what was once the attic. But the basic structure of the Cottage has remained unchanged, and it is still a functional writer's retreat.

In our spacious living room with windows overlooking the valley, my wife has placed some fine eighteenth-century French country pieces, including a huge buffet that reaches to the ceiling. (This furniture came from her family's country house outside Paris, which was recently sold.)

"You will no doubt now be inspired to write poems about yellow violets, as Bryant did," Louis Untermeyer told me when I acquired this house. I haven't yet, but I have written poems here on a variety of subjects. There are many ghosts but they all seem to be friendly ones; this is a wonderful place to work. A few years ago my wife and stepson acquired the 200 acres across the road that were originally part of the property. I like to think that William Cullen Bryant, as well as the many writers who have followed him on these premises, would have approved of the way they are used.

Padraic Colum, who once occupied the house, was one of our first guests. When he came to dinner, he said, "Mary [his wife] was so bored when we lived here that she threw a plate out the window." He stood on the porch looking out into the field as if the plate were still there. (Mary Colum was a critic and perhaps that accounts for her being bored. None of the poets and fiction writers who have stayed here has ever mentioned boredom.)

William Cullen Bryant was the first American poet to be appreciated by readers outside the United States. It seems natural then that we should continue a tradition of having writers here from all over the world. One of the seemingly endless ironies connected with the Bryant Cottage is that, like Harriet Moody before her, Sonja once had a catering business. And so she has maintained the other tradition, with more adequate equipment than was available to Mrs. Moody and a Parisian touch that the Chicago lady may have lacked, of providing visiting writers with excellent food.

Andrei Voznesensky, the Russian poet whose poems I have translated, spent Thanksgiving with us not long ago in Cummington. He felt very much at home in our woods, not unlike those at Peredelkino, the writers' colony outside Moscow where he lives and where we have visited him. He was interested to learn that there is a type of black birch tree here that does not exist on his home ground. But then, why shouldn't it exist here? This is, we knew from the moment we first saw it, a very special place.

JOHN HOLLANDER

William Cullen Bryant as Poet

THE FIGURES OF WILLIAM CULLEN BRYANT and Thomas Cole stand over a gorge in the Catskills, the "Kindred Spirits" of their friend Asher B. Durand's painting of that name. Cole is expounding, his long painter's brush at rest against his palette, pointing out for the viewer of the painting the rock formation across the gorge — the kind, indeed, that it was Cole's delight to paint. Bryant stands deep in meditation. But in a deeper sense, poet, painter and the scene that surrounds them are all engaged in another sort of mutual interpretation: the spirits of language and art both half-perceive and half-create the vision of the natural sublime before them. They also present us with a parable of American romanticism.

Bryant is our first poet of nature, recapitulating even in the earliest years of his work the movement from the passive speculations of a poetic derived from the later eighteenth-century poets of sensibility, to a meditative mode in which the mind is more actively engaged in intercourse with the natural emblems and figures of itself. Though lacking the mighty poetic intellect and cataclysmic originating power of an Emerson, Bryant nonetheless preceded him in transplanting imaginative seeds that would not fall on barren ground. "He's a Cowper condensed, with no craziness bitten,/And the advantage that Wordsworth before him had written," jingled James Russell Lowell: and yet to have responded to a reading of Wordsworth — as the testimony of the successive drafts of "Thanatopsis" assures us he did — was as crucial for its moment in the history of American

poetry as the responses of Wyatt, and particularly Surrey, to Pe-
trarch were for the literature of England, or as Hawthorne's to
Spenser would be later on.

Thomas Cole's presence in Durand's painting is also of signifi-
cance for the American imagination. Cole had encountered the ro-
mantic tableaux of John Martin (and, after going abroad, German
romantic painting as well), but produced a major oeuvre of his own
kind of mythological landscape. In groups of paintings like *The
Voyage of Life, Past and Present,* & *The Course of Empire* he had
imprinted upon European conventions of landscape painting new
versions of the picturesque and the sublime. He gave meaning to
American scenery by means of a poetic narrative of cyclic fable and
moral journey. But it was Cole's romantic landscapes that allowed
followers like Durand, Cropsey, Kensett — and even Albert Bier-
stadt and Frederick Church later on — to naturalize the narrative
scenes and patterns, and reinvest with metaphoric significance the
structures of uninhabited natural scene. In this way, Cole not only
kept — as Bryant urged him to do in a sonnet written for the painter's
departure on a voyage to Europe — "that wilder [i.e., American]
image bright" but, indeed, first illuminated it.

Bryant's own vision of nature is more immediately like that of the
later Hudson River School painters than like Cole's. And yet the
Spenserian stanzas of his Harvard Phi Beta Kappa poem of 1821,
"The Ages," suggest the mode of poetic history revealed in Cole's
The Course of Empire sequence. Stanzas 28–29 contemplate a bright
bay full of the sails of commercial shipping, observing that there,
once, "The savage urged his skiff like wild bird on the wing." The
next two stanzas move through ironies going far beyond any eigh-
teenth-century vision of the nobility of savagery, even as they avoid
the entrepreneurial self-satisfaction of manifest destiny, erasing his-
torical knowledge and perhaps sentimentalizing relics:

There stood the Indian hamlet, there the lake
Spread its blue sheet that flashed with many an oar,
Where the brown otter plunged him from the brake,
And the deer drank; as the light gale flew o'er,
The twinkling maize-field rustled on the shore;
And while that spot, so wild, so lone, so fair,
A look of glad and guiltless beauty wore,
And peace was on the earth and in the air,
The warrior lit the pile, and bound his captive there.

Not unavenged — the foeman from the wood
Beheld the deed, and when midnight shade
Was stillest, gorged his battle-axe with blood;
All died — the wailing babe — the shrinking maid —
And in the flood of fire that scaled the glade,
The roofs went down; but deep the silence grew,
When on the dewy woods the day-beam played;
No more the cabin-smokes rose wreathed and blue,
And ever, by their lake, lay moored the bark canoe.

All of "The Ages" is not up to this; and indeed, the difference is generally great between Bryant's best poetry and the indifferent verse of his later years. While a student at Williams College, reading law in Massachusetts and then practicing it with limited success and satisfaction, he conceived his best work. After he moved to New York City in 1825 to function there as a Man of Letters, and particularly after he became editor of the important New York *Evening Post* in 1829, Bryant's power as a true poet fell off. We can be more grateful for his 1844 editorial proposing that "a tract of beautiful woodland" at that time "on the road to Harlem" be set aside for a public park "to match Regent's Park or the Prater" (the eventual Central Park) than we can for most of what he wrote in verse after the 1830s (an exception is "A Rain-Dream" of 1854). Of a severely pruned list of his truly fine poems, the first five were published in a collection by 1821. I should say that the following represent the oeuvre that, the remarkable felicities of Freneau and the passionate purity of Bradstreet aside, makes Bryant our first true poet: "Thanatopsis"; "To a Waterfowl"; "Inscription for the Entrance to a Wood"; "Green River"; "The Ages"; "A Winter Piece"; the wonderful "Summer Wind"; "Autumn Woods"; "A Forest Hymn"; "June"; "To the Fringed Gentian"; the sonnet to Cole, "A Scene on the Banks of the Hudson"; "The Conjugation of Venus and Jupiter"; "The Prairies"; "Earth"; "The Snow-Shower"; and "A Rain-Dream."

The blank-verse translation of Homer to which Bryant devoted many of his later mornings is somewhat flat, possessing some of the more dubious virtues of "readability," but its projection evidences traces of its author's somewhat surprising lifelong admiration of Pope (even if its execution owes more to Cowper). Little wit appears in Bryant's verse (save for one juvenile effort), although his generally libertarian – but by no means prematurely abolitionist – *Evening Post* editorials can be quite sharp at times. Bryant was ideologically unadventurous and intellectually unenterprising. Lowell's *Fable for Critics* depicts him in his early fifties, shortly before the time of Durand's painting, as being cold and somewhat distant ("There's no doubt that he stands in complete iceolation"). But it never seems to have been the life of the mind to which Bryant had retreated. Indeed, the inability to build further on his earlier vision, with that power of poetic intellect which interprets the very grounds on which previous intuitions have been received, is what finally limits him as an American poet, when compared with the giants of his century – Emerson, Whitman, Dickinson.

But as a craftsman he explored a host of forms and took poetic structure very seriously, writing as early as 1819 an essay on trisyllabic feet in iambic verse, partly, perhaps, to justify his own neoaccentual leanings, which produced the lovely "Green River":

> As if the bright fringe of herbs on its brink
> Had given their stain to the waves they drink;
> And they, whose meadows it murmurs through,
> Have named the stream from its own fair hue.

(The stream sounds like a tributary to Robert Frost's "West Running Brook.") His deployment of a quatrain that Robert Southey had used earlier (as I am informed by Mr. William Cullen Bryant II) in "To a Waterfowl" — a poem Matthew Arnold and Hartley Coleridge once agreed was the best short poem in English — reorganizes the tetrameter quatrain into a new species of lyric strophe that Horace never knew, but that seemed somehow always to have existed. And yet it is no mere ingenuity of verse, but a creation of poetry. The opening and closing lines, contrasting with the middle lines in length as well as in the way by which they coincide or not with syntactic units, constantly remind us of the poem's set tropes of flight, paths, distance, & ultimately significant journeying. The opening question —

> Whither, midst falling dew,
> While glow the heavens with the last steps of day
> Far, through their rosy depths, dost thou pursue
> Thy solitary way?

— and the closing lesson read from the emblem of contemplating the bird's flight —

> He who, from zone to zone,
> Guides through the boundless sky thy certain flight,
> In the long way that I must tread alone
> Will lead my steps aright.

interpret the form of their utterance even as they give meaning to the object of the invocation. Bryant never wrote better than he did in early poems like this one, and we might apply to him — *mutatis mutandis* to himself and his life of letters and journalism in New York — the rest of the caveat he urged on Cole's imagination, not to become too Europeanized as he encountered

> everywhere the race of men.
> Paths, homes, graves, ruins, from the lowest glen
> To where life shrinks from the fierce Alpine air.
> Gaze on them, till the tears shall dim thy sight,
> But keep that earlier, wilder image bright.

AARON KRAMER

William Cullen Bryant as Poet of Liberty

MAY 29, 1878. Central Park, New York. A likeness of Mazzini, Italy's supreme patriot, is being unveiled. William Cullen Bryant delivers the main address. In the past he has been chief orator at the dedication of other Central Park statues: to Samuel Morse, Walter Scott, Shakespeare. World poet of liberation and justice for sixty years, editor of the liberal New York *Evening Post* for half a century, Bryant — even more than usual — thrills the crowd today with his eloquence, makes them forget an intolerable sun. His final words to the statue sweep through them:

> Image of the illustrious champion of civil and religious liberty, cast in enduring bronze to typify the imperishable renown of thy original, remain for ages yet to come where we place thee, in this resort of millions! Remain till the day shall dawn, far distant though it may be, when the rights and duties of human brotherhood shall be acknowledged by all the races of mankind!

Editor's Note: This commentary is an edited transcript of a radio program, originally titled "William Cullen Bryant: A Centenary Tribute," broadcast twice on WNYC's *Spoken Words* series on June 12, 1978. The section on Bryant as poet of nature, a subject treated elsewhere in this book, has been deleted, and the author, to conserve space, has condensed quotations from Bryant's poetry. Time limitations placed upon him by the radio format also required exclusion of "such worthy political expressions" as "The Antiquity of Freedom," "A Bright Day," "Italy," the conclusion of "Among the Trees," and these relevant lines from the Roslyn poem "The Planting of the Apple-Tree":

> Oh, when its aged branches throw
> Thin shadows on the ground below,
> Shall fraud and force and iron will
> Oppress the weak and helpless still?

But the heat of the day takes its toll. Leaning on the arm of General Wilson, the 83-year-old poet reaches his friend's residence on East 74th Street, collapses, strikes his head on the steps. For two weeks a shocked nation watches one of its authentic giants ebb into unconsciousness. June 12th is a day of universal mourning. In the decades that follow, new styles, new tastes push aside long-dominant names. Whitman, Melville, Emily Dickinson, unknown or rejected during the heyday of Bryant, Longfellow, & Whittier, are now ranked as the prime spokesmen of the century. Entranced by generation after generation of powerful new voices, critics place Bryant in a remote limbo, dangerously close to oblivion. "Thanatopsis" and "To a Waterfowl" may still be praised and anthologized, but grudgingly, patronizingly.

The centennial of a great man's death is as good a time as any to reassess his career. Surely, selections from Bryant's pure and often historic prose: editorials, addresses, essays, letters, especially a marvelous series from Europe in which he shares his impressions with the readers of the *Evening Post*, deserve a full, separate focus. Attention should also be given to his masterly renderings from Spanish, German, French, Portuguese, and his crowning later achievements: translations of the *Iliad* and *Odyssey*. This broadcast, however, limits itself to two aspects of Bryant's genius: as celebrant of nature . . . and as clarion of liberty — at home no less than abroad.

His best-loved Indian poems are elegiac; notable among them is
the 1824 "Monument Mountain," which retells an ancient legend
of a maiden's incestuous love for her cousin. "An Indian at the
Burial Place of His Fathers" was written about the same time, but
is as indignant as the other is gentle:

> They waste us — ay — like April snow
>   In the warm noon, we shrink away;
> And fast they follow, as we go
>   Toward the setting day —
> Till they shall fill the land, and we
> Are driven into the Western sea.
>
> But I behold a fearful sign,
>   To which the white men's eyes are blind;
> Their race may vanish hence, like mine,
>   And leave no trace behind . . .
> The realm our tribes are crushed to get
> May be a barren desert yet.

That year, with the same moral fervor, Bryant addressed other
social issues as well. The final passages of "After a Tempest" express
the identical yearning for peace that was to spark Longfellow's
"Arsenal at Springfield" twenty years later:

> I looked, and thought the quiet of the scene
> An emblem of the peace that yet shall be,
> When o'er earth's continents, and isles between,
> The noise of war shall cease from sea to sea,
> And married nations dwell in harmony:
> When millions, crouching in the dust to one,
> No more shall beg their lives on bended knee . . .
>
> Too long, at clash of arms amid her bowers
> And pools of blood, the earth has stood aghast . . .
> Lo, the clouds roll away — they break — they fly,
> And, like the glorious light of summer, cast
> O'er the wide landscape from the embracing sky,
> On all the peaceful world the smile of heaven shall lie.

Bryant's poems inspired by Greece's nine-year revolt against Tur-
key match the fervor if not the greatness of Shelley's drama *Hellas*
and Byron's personal heroism. One of his most restrained yet moving
is "The Massacre at Scio," composed after an unspeakable butchery
by Turkish troops on the island claimed as Homer's birthplace:

> Weep not for Scio's children slain;
>   Their blood, by Turkish falchions shed,
> Sends not its cry to Heaven in vain
>   For vengeance on the murderer's head.
>
> Though high the warm red torrent ran
>   Between the flames that lit the sky,
> Yet, for each drop, an arméd man
>   Shall rise, to free the land, or die.

Even more passionate is "The Conjunction of Jupiter and Venus,"
declaring his disgust at the indifference of the world toward Greece's
agony. Here are the concluding passages:

> Hapless Greece!
> Enough of blood has wet thy rocks, and stained
> Thy rivers; deep enough thy chains have worn
> Their links into thy flesh . . .
> Thine is a war for liberty, and thou
> Must fight it single-handed. The old world
> Looks coldly on the murderers of thy race,
> And leaves thee to the struggle; and the new, —
> I fear me thou couldst tell a shameful tale
> Of fraud and lust of gain . . . Yet thy wrongs
> Shall put new strength into thy heart and hand,
> And God and thy good sword shall yet work out,
> For thee, a terrible deliverance.

"William Tell," a product of the same period, is worthy of consid-
eration along with Wordsworth's "Toussaint L'Ouverture" and

Byron's "Chillon" among the noblest sonnets on liberty in the
English language:

> Chains may subdue the feeble spirit, but thee,
>   TELL, of the iron heart! they could not tame!
>   For thou wert of the mountains; they proclaim
> The everlasting creed of liberty.
> That creed is written on the untrampled snow,
>   Thundered by torrents which no power can hold,
>   Save that of God, when He sends forth His cold,
> And breathed by winds that through the free heaven blow.
> Thou, while thy prison-walls were dark around,
>   Didst meditate the lesson Nature taught,
>   And to thy brief captivity was brought
> A vision of thy Switzerland unbound.
>   The bitter cup they mingled, strengthened thee
>   For the great work to set thy country free.

Bryant's intense involvement in the worldwide battle for liberty
never slackened. "A Brighter Day," written at 73, and "Christmas
in 1875," written at 81, are as stirring as any of his youthful verses
on this theme. But it is easier to defy an overseas oppressor than
those at home. Bryant never made peace with American tyranny,
which defiled the dream of the *Mayflower* colonists from whom he
was directly descended on both sides.

As editor-in-chief of the New York *Evening Post*, he championed
the rights of workingmen to form unions, bargain collectively, and
strike — extraordinary concepts for that time, causing many firms to
withdraw as advertisers. He advocated the destruction of debtor
laws, the abolition of slavery. He backed Andrew Jackson and the
attack on the Bank of the United States, currency regulations that
favored the have-nots, prison reforms. In stinging editorials he de-
nounced the mob spirit that hounded abolition-editor Birney in
Cincinnati in 1836 and martyred Lovejoy in Alton, Illinois a year
later. In 1848 he bolted the Democratic Party for betraying Jackson's

principles, and joined the Free-Soilers, the radical Barn-Burners. He condemned the Fugitive Slave Law as "the most ruffianly act ever authorized by a deliberative assembly," and the Dred Scott Decision as "a disgrace." He defended John Brown as one of the martyrs and heroes of history. He helped organize the Republican Party in 1855, and headed its militant anti-slavery wing in New York. He presided at Lincoln's great Cooper Union address in 1860, campaigned vigorously for his election and re-election, lashed out repeatedly at the Copperheads, including New York's governor and other high officials. Through his high moral and literary standards he lifted the New York *Evening Post* to a position of greatness in the history of American journalism.

In 1837, the year of Lovejoy's martyrdom and of mob actions in New York against his own editorship, he wrote "The Battlefield":

> A friendless warfare! lingering long
>   Through weary day and weary year,
> A wild and many-weaponed throng
>   Hang on thy front, and flank, and rear.
>
> Yet nerve thy spirit to the proof,
>   And blench not at thy chosen lot.
> The timid good may stand aloof,
>   The sage may frown — yet faint thou not . . .
>
> Truth, crushed to earth, shall rise again;
>   The eternal years of God are hers;
> But Error, wounded, writhes in pain,
>   And dies among his worshippers . . .
>
> Another hand thy sword shall wield,
>   Another hand the standard wave,
> Till from the trumpet's mouth is pealed
>   The blast of triumph o'er thy grave.

Bryant's once widely-loved battle-cries of 1861 have fallen into

oblivion, as Whitman's *Drum-Taps* have risen to first place among
the poems of the Civil War. But "Our Country's Call" still has the
power to recruit one's imagination:

> Lay down the axe; fling by the spade;
>   Leave in its track the toiling plough;
> The rifle and the bayonet-blade
>   For arms like yours were fitter now . . .
> Our country calls; away! away!
>   To where the blood-stream blots the green.
> Strike to defend the gentlest sway
>   That Time in all his course has seen . . .
>
> Few, few were they whose swords of old
>   Won the fair land in which we dwell;
> But we are many, we who hold
>   The grim resolve to guard it well.
> Strike, for that broad and goodly land,
>   Blow after blow, till men shall see
> That Might and Right move hand in hand,
>   And glorious must their triumph be!

"The Death of Lincoln" expressed the national grief in April,
1865. This hymn has been altogether swept aside by the splendor
which we are now able to appreciate in "When Lilacs Last in the
Dooryard Bloom'd." But the spare, pure lines of Bryant's poem
deserve a hearing:

> Oh, slow to smite and swift to spare,
>   Gentle and merciful and just!
> Who, in the fear of God, didst bear
>   The sword of power, a nation's trust!
>
> In sorrow by thy bier we stand,
>   Amid the awe that hushes all,
> And speak the anguish of a land
>   That shook with horror at thy fall.
>
> Thy task is done; the bond are free:
>   We bear thee to an honored grave,

Whose proudest monument shall be
  The broken fetters of the slave . . .

"The Death of Slavery," a remarkable burst of exuberance for a
man of 72, defines with as much force as we can find in his best
editorials and speeches, Bryant's lifelong hatred of that institution:

Great as thou wert, and feared from shore to shore,
  The wrath of Heaven o'ertook thee in thy pride;
Thou sit'st a ghastly shadow; by thy side
  Thy once strong arms hang nerveless evermore . . .

Well was thy doom deserved; thou didst not spare
  Life's tenderest ties, but cruelly didst part
  Husband and wife, and from the mother's heart
Didst wrest her children, deaf to shriek and prayer;
    Thy inner lair became
    The haunt of guilty shame;
Thy lash dropped blood; the murderer, at thy side,
  Showed his red hands, nor feared the vengeance due.
Thou didst sow earth with crimes, and, far and wide,
  A harvest of uncounted miseries grew,
Until the measure of thy sins at last
Was full, and then the avenging bolt was cast! . . .

I do want to go back to an elegy of 1839. In that year the embattled
co-editor of the *Evening Post*, William Leggett, died at the age of 38.
This little poem characterizes Bryant as well; and I believe the con-
cluding stanzas deserve to stand as the final word on William Cullen
Bryant:

The words of fire that from his pen
  Were flung upon the fervid page,
Still move, still shake the hearts of men,
  Amid a cold and coward age.

His love of truth, too warm, too strong
  For Hope or Fear to chain or chill,
His hate of tyranny and wrong,
  Burn in the breasts he kindled still.

ROBERT MORGAN

Bryant's Solitary Glimpse of Paradise

BRYANT IS THE FIRST AMERICAN POET because he is the first to have glanced at Paradise. His Eden is more dignified and classical than the imaginary gardens of Poe, Emerson, Thoreau, Whitman, and Dickinson, but he saw an authentic vision of vast spaces and silence in which a single waterfowl drifted, and forests soughed hymns to be overheard by the solitary, and the ground was haunted and sacred with the memory of primeval dead. Wherever he looked, in his youth, in his best poems, there was the Eden-glimmer that was the essence of our first poetry.

Between the wilderness and the Enlightenment, between the church clearing and the hunting woods, at the edge of the industrial age, Bryant struck his new note. Just when the savage and the true wilderness were almost gone from New England, and the faith that opposed them waning, he glanced into the forest shadows and found dignity and confidence, a stoic joy. Looking closely at the earth around him he saw a moral language of process, consonant with deism, inspiring trust, comfort, in the rational mind.

After the terror and exclusions of Calvinism, what an assurance to see the infinite cycles of decay and growth, incorporating human compost in fertile progression. Most great poems touch somehow the figure of resurrection, but "Thanatopsis" succeeds through its noble music in evoking communion through death and collective loss. The wilderness and nature *are* death, but mind and imagination are comforted by nature's parallels with deity. Rather than damnation or sainthood, there is the infallible grace of community with all. Eternity and the future are transfigured beneath our feet.

Bryant is the first distinctive American poetic voice, and the first luminist. When he speaks he overcomes inherited fear through elevation and stability, echoing the romantics of the century before, but also glimpsing the freedom and radiance of a new world. He speaks of exhilarating distances, and the thrill of aloneness that Boone and Audubon, Bartram and Michaux, had known before him. He is the poet of childhood and sunsets, of sowing and orchards, of the home-made line he fashioned from the devotional poems and hymns he was familiar with, and which he subverted to serve his new vision. It is appropriate that he touched his note when young and never found another, for he is the youthful poet of a young country. His best poems seem both old and new at once, reflecting his wise revisions and the rural, half-English world that nurtured him. If his accent still reminds us of Gray and Collins at times, it suggests also the fresh forests and rivers and skies around him, and the gleam of heaven within the transience. The virgin woods flower over the strata of heaped dead in the language, in the reaches of imaginative memory. If his homiletic tone seems wrong to our ears, his observation and music are still accurate. Without its last stanza "To a Waterfowl" may seem a more perfect lyric to our taste, a limpid song of openness and solitude, but it would not be the poem that Bryant meant, and it would not be the sweet vision of poise and aspiration the youthful, somewhat awkward America of his time responded to and loved.

RICHARD ELMAN

Yvor Winters, Wallace Stevens, and "Thanatopsis"

IT WAS YVOR WINTERS in the nineteen-fifties at Stanford, as I recall, who taught me to appreciate Cullen Bryant's "Thanatopsis." The grand curmudgeon liked very little American poetry, aside from Emily Dickinson and Robinson and the work of his students, but he had ambiguous, if not complicated, responses to Wallace Stevens; and it was in connection with Stevens that Winters pointed out that "Sunday Morning" was the best blank verse since "Thanatopsis." He asked us to read the poem carefully, if we never had, study the movement of the verses, and notice the resemblances: "When thoughts/Of the last bitter hour come like a blight/Over thy spirit, and sad images . . ."

I entered "that mysterious realm, where each shall take/His chamber in the silent halls of death" with a considerable reluctance. True enough, Bryant's vision was a good deal more coherent than Stevens', but also more grim, almost leaden, it seemed to me. Winters was always recommending these grim leaden figures to supplant my heroes. He called Whitman a "second-rater absolutely" and Hart Crane was discussed in terms of his homosexuality, not necessarily his poetry. Was the great Yvor, whom I then hated and feared, using Bryant to reproach Stevens for his cosmopolite sophistications, or sophistries? I loved "Sunday Morning" and so did Winters, he claimed, adjourning his love for the poet only after the first couple of volumes began to produce work of a feckless "hedonism."

With Winters you never knew if he really believed "Thanatopsis" was the only truly great American poem of the first half of the nineteenth century, or if that was a way of telling his scholarly and critical friends in American Studies et cetera that they wouldn't know their own toe if they were eating it.

At various times Winters also used "Thanatopsis" to beat up on the blank verse of T. S. Eliot, and Hart Crane, and even Robert Lowell, so it, eventually, became a sort of obligation with me to know and remember the poem, for its easy movement of the caesura, and its variable imagery, its diction which is never fustian nor inverted:

> The hills
> Rock ribbed and ancient as the sun, — the vales
> Stretching in pensive quietness between;
> The venerable woods — rivers that move
> In majesty, and the complaining brooks
> That make the meadows green; and, poured round all,
> Old Ocean's grey and melancholy waste, —

Bryant was first, last and always an editorial writer, so he editorialized a bit with words like "venerable," "majesty," "melancholy," but he does manage to convince us with wonder and power of the process whereby the earth is "the great tomb of man." Bryant's poem has considerable force as an elegant, though truistic, statement about death.

Winters is long ago buried in that great tomb, and probably some of the earth Bryant was evoking is now neither cemetery nor wilderness but a housing tract. And, perhaps, on warm Sunday mornings, one of the local ladies takes coffee in her peignoir on the patio, and "dreams a little of that dark catastrophe." Would it comfort her to know that "matron, and maid/And the sweet babe, and the greyheaded man —/Shall one by one be gathered to thy side . . . "?

RICHARD EBERHART

Memory of Learning Bryant's "Thanatopsis" in Youth

WHEN I WAS ABOUT FIFTEEN OR SIXTEEN in the old red brick high
school at Austin, Minnesota, our teacher asked the class to write a
poem. I went home and found in our library the works of Alfred
Lord Tennyson which I devoured with fascination and immediate
enthusiasm, falling in love with the musicality of his lines and the
perfection of his rhymes. I imitated Tennyson and instead of bring-
ing one poem to class, as did my classmates, I always brought in
several, maybe even half a dozen. It was a sheer joy to write lines of
verse similar to the joy of running the hundred-yard dash.

At this time I encountered Bryant's "Thanatopsis" and learned
it by heart. I used to repeat it over and over with total absorption.
It has been with me ever since. I knew nothing of his life at the time
and did not know other poems of his. The magnificent lines were
engraved on my mind. The other night I partly awoke and the whole
poem came to me almost intact sixty-five years later. Later in college
I studied the problem of the ending and had such severity of judg-
ment that I thought these added lines were wrong. After decades I
concluded that they were justified, they added to the totality of the
experience.

I do not know when I first read "To a Waterfowl" and "To a
Fringed Gentian," which I enjoyed, but for reasons unknown was
not compelled to learn them by heart. "Thanatopsis" remains as a
profound experience of poetry when I was very young. Its power
has not diminished with time.

Was it not Pound who said that to be remembered a poet must have two, meaning at least two, memorable poems? You do not have to read all of Marvell but everybody knows his "Coy Mistress" and "The Garden." Bryant wrote one great poem and he wrote it when he was very young. Pound's dictum should be revised downward in his case.

PAUL ENGLE

Two Long Island Voices Heard in the Heartland

THERE IS A THEORY about American poetry, that it is divided into two extremes, the pale face and the redskin. Late examples are Carl Sandburg as the poet of violence, the worker in the steel mill drowning in the hot furnace, the hard-handed farmer husking his corn, the redskin. The paleface was T. S. Eliot, writing about the over-refined Prufrock, walking through streets as twisted as his mind, "Where the evening is spread out against the sky/Like a patient etherized upon a table." The tough guy and the effete, the hard and the gentle.

Long Island had precisely those extremes. It is astonishing to find two poets so close together in time and place, yet so far apart in theme, tone, rhythm, form, personal life, career, voice. It is an amazing and enriching aspect of American literature that two poets should have lived within so few miles and so few years of each other, as William Cullen Bryant and Walt Whitman.

"To be a brother to the insensible rock," as Bryant phrased it, was my childhood ambition. Although I haunted libraries, I also haunted the limestone cliffs, once an ocean bottom with its Devonian fossils which I collected along with the intricate corals frozen in design under the cornfields, along the Cedar, Iowa, and Wapsipinicon Rivers. Just as Thoreau wrote about "insulting June," Bryant wrote about "the complaining brooks." Why were they complaining in their busy life making the meadows green, sheltering fish, whispering over stones, logs, sand? Bryant's poetry had little complaining in it, but the word in this line is shrewd. Bryant was not always that tough in his vocabulary.

Although Whitman made me long to spend a day on the Brooklyn

Ferry and Longfellow made me want to turn myself into an Indian, when I read "Thanatopsis" it did not make me yearn to die, attractive as Bryant made the idea. Since I was a teenage boy in vigorous health, my dreams were often lively and unrepeatable; certainly, I did not feel "Like one who wraps the drapery of his couch/About him, and lies down to pleasant dreams." I preferred my own shameful dreams. Although I admired the line, "Old Ocean's gray and melancholy waste," I had a different view of those who might "make their bed with thee." Nor did I feel myself "the quarry-slave at night,/Scourged to his dungeon." I was a healthy, free worker who at night went to his narrow bedroom whose walls were hung with hummingbird nests, arrowheads, picture cards of famous baseball players, and photos of my white collie dog.

Even though Bryant wrote many of his more famous poems in western Massachusetts, all of his lines about nature, the waterfowl, the lake, the river, the ocean (above all, the ocean) made me feel that I should move to Long Island with the turbulent Atlantic on two sides, the salty Sound on another and a "river" on the fourth. Above all, the sea, the sea. In "The Prairies" he said of that landscape that it looked

> As if the ocean, in his gentlest swell,
> Stood still, with all his rounded billows fixed,
> And motionless forever . . .

Whitman also made me want to settle down on Long Island, where the salt water is never far away and one can reach Montauk quickly, where one could be "a simple separate person" living "all summer in the sound of the sea . . . Over the hoarse surging of the sea." Like most good ol' Iowa boys, I found the ocean as irresistible (so many Midwestern men in the U.S. Navy, even admirals!) as Whitman did.

Both Bryant and Whitman paid their deepest respect to death. It was Walt who combined the two themes of ocean and death in one poem, "Out of the Cradle Endlessly Rocking":

> Whereto answering the sea,
> Delaying not, hurrying not
> Whisper'd me through the night, and very plainly before daybreak,
> Lisp'd to me the low and delicious word death, . . .
> Hissing melodious, neither like the bird nor like my arous'd child's heart,
> But edging near as privately for me rustling at my feet,
> Creeping thence steadily up to my ears and laving me softly all over,
> Death, death, death, death, death.

Surely Whitman's "When Lilacs Last in the Dooryard Bloom'd" is the greatest American poem on death, and as a kid I was enchanted to find that Whitman joined the oceans with my own Midwest:

> Sea winds blown from east and west,
> Blown from the Eastern sea and blown from the Western sea, till there on
>   the prairies meeting . . .

How could these two poets, so different in lives, in personalities, in language, have had such themes in common? In their portraits, these two death-haunted poets seem life-rejoicing, yet their great poems are of death, however different their language, rhythm, lives.

Bryant and Whitman were close observers of the human and natural life of Long Island, and Whitman's use of the lilac as an important image was especially evocative for me in the Midwest. We had lilacs in our yard in Cedar Rapids. Each Memorial Day we picked them and put their purple-violet-blue blossoms, with their odor sweet as no other flower's, on the graves of our family, on the grave of grandpa, Civil War cavalryman and gentle man (or gentleman), of little Paul, my uncle who died at eight of a mysterious sudden shock, of old mysterious Engle grandma whom none of us had ever seen and her husband we never knew, who abandoned family and was last seen riding a wild horse across the state border in the Oklahoma land rush. Whitman wrote a line which I recognized in the sorrow of the family: "I leave thee lilac with heart-shaped leaves."

In yearning to leave Iowa for Long Island, I had to confront the two American literary traditions. Bryant was obviously the paleface, the genteel poet of soft lines (with some hard phrases), the literary type. Whitman was obviously the voice of the "barbaric yawp," the common man writing uncommonly about the common man. How could a small area within a small Island contain two such contrary poets? Whereas Bryant wrote "thou," Whitman wrote "you." Why did Bryant put an apostrophe " ' " in place of the usual "e" in so many words? Was this literary pretension? Bryant, the more conventionally literary poet of the two, did not honor contemporary usage. In brief, the Long Island where Bryant and Whitman lived also contained the wild extremes of American literature.

In Iowa, that confused me. Should I be a respectable poet like Bryant, full of sensibility expressed in conventional words? Or should I be an eccentric (for his times), peculiar celebrator of the same nature about which Bryant wrote, but write in a shouting, not a genteel, voice — Whitman? Or take the brisk attitude toward reality of Emily Dickinson: "I'd toss it yonder like a rind/And taste eternity." Or should I attempt the grotesque image of Oliver Wendell Holmes — "Her hair drooped round her pallid cheeks, like seawood on a clam"? Or Emerson's amazing image about wine — "Or like the Atlantic streams, which run/When the South Sea calls."

Although I have gathered horseshoe crabs in Gardiner's Bay with my daughters, and swum in the great surf of October off Amagansett beach, and crossed Long Island Sound by ferry, swum in the Club pool at East Hampton and walked the glittering sands at Sands

Point, I never made the move to Long Island. I once thought of
living halfway between the Whitman and Bryant houses, hoping
that geography would solve my writing problems.

So I remained (save for years in Europe and Asia), happily living
in Iowa where I first read Bryant and Whitman. One day I will visit
the Bryant and Whitman houses within a few hours, properly hum-
bled by the two Long Islanders who kept alive that poetic energy
whose lightning broke over the Iowa silos.

NORBERT KRAPF

Walking with Walt Whitman & William Cullen Bryant:
A Fantasy

YOU'RE IN A WOODS on a hillside overlooking a lake and a bay.
Winds through the oaks, sun on the water. Standing on gravel
at a bend in a washed-out lane, you look out over another century.
Two bearded poets, one a quarter of a century older, shorter,
and neater, stroll around a spring-fed lake. You can almost hear
their boots squish in the marshy grass. The older one points out
his prize copper beech, Japanese maples, ancient black walnut,
mound of rhododendron, and watercress along the brook over-
flowing into the bay. He motions toward the boat house, his guest
nods, and they row across clear water. As they disembark, the
younger poet asks a question as he points at a gothic mill, then

glances back at the lake as they climb stairs to the eighteenth-century Quaker farmhouse. They sit on a bench in a formal boxwood garden and listen to water spill out of a fountain. The younger poet stands up to watch a Canada goose and her five goslings wobble past a rabbit on the lawn slanting toward the bay. When the shadows touch on the surface of the lake below, the older poet puts his hands on the shoulder of the younger, guides him onto the latticed piazza into the farmhouse.

You find yourself alone again in the woods that used to belong to the older poet. Sun on your face, wind in your beard, you read aloud to yourself these lines the younger poet wrote in his seventies:

(For song, issuing from its birth-place, after fulfillment, wandering,
  Reck'd or unreck'd, duly with love returns.)

You look up and see a full sail on the Sound and know these are now your poets, your woods, your sun, wind, and water; and this is your place.

II

Underground Tide:
Poems

NORBERT KRAPF

By the Waters of Cedarmere

(for William Stafford)

I
How the clear water
spilling over from

the spring-fed lake
the Roslyn poet

gazed into a cen-
tury or so ago

still sings
syllables of joy

over small rocks
reflecting sunlight

green watercress
tethered to the bank

floats once again
in April flux

a rabbit hops
into the shade

of a blue spruce
along Hempstead Bay

and cocks his ears
when I whistle

as the boy I was
did in Indiana woods

my son babbles
notes in your arms

like the ones you
draw out of the quiet

of the earth
far to the West

and my daughter
frisking ahead

stoops to pick up
a nest of nickles

someone left in
last year's leaves

and floats a cry
back across the waters.

II
As we climb up the hill
beneath the copper beech

planted beside the lake by
the poet who knelt in groves

we stop to look at
the ancient silver maple

that cracked, twisted,
and crashed to earth

in an early spring storm.
In the nearby eighteenth-century

Quaker farmhouse in which
the old poet translated

Homer's *Iliad* and *Odyssey*,
dust filters to the floor

on rays of sunlight.
Here at eye level buds

as red as raspberries
cluster on every branch.

"Look at that," you say,
"it still won't stop!"

Yes, and rhubarb red
peony shafts rise up

out of the brown lawn
and curl at the tip.

III
In the Bryant family
plot in Roslyn Cemetery

we walk around
the granite obelisk

beside the big beech
onto which people who

do not love poetry
but claim they love

one another have
carved rude initials

in interlocking hearts.
Prickly beechnut shells

crunch beneath our shoes.
Elizabeth munches a pear

at our side while Daniel
sleeps in the car.

You step toward
the stump of an oak

standing in a halo
of undarkened sawdust.

"We can count the rings,"
you say,   and press

a wide-open hand across
a Great Plains of sunset-

red rings and cracks.
"About 110 years," you

reckon. So the acorn sprouted
up out of this earth a few

years before the gray-bearded
poet settled back into it.

In a voice so soft
and measured it could have

been seeping up out
of the earth or sifting

down from the budding
beech you say: "So he

looked out over this
beautiful place and said:

To him who in the love
of Nature holds communion

with her visible forms, she
speaks a various language . . ."

I V
High in the woods
where he cleared a path

and vistas to the water
with his sickly wife

we look back down on
lake, farmhouse, bay.

We follow the path to
a derelict board-and-batten

cottage the rich journalist–
poet built for a friend.

Rot snakes around the foundation.
A sapling pokes out of a brick

chimney just above
the slate roof. Weeds

have staked a good claim.
Although the damp seems

almost impossible to dislodge,
we imagine a good life

behind the walls, hope
for a steady restoration.

Somewhere in a farmhouse
in the Berkshires, in southern

Indiana hills, on the Great
Plains, or in the mountains

of the West, someone kindles
and stokes a fire. Somewhere

a baby is always being born
as someone else dies. Buds

open in the woods, acorns
sprout after the storm

twists and pulls an ancient
giant earthward. Someone

to whom our backs must
be turned always follows

along the path. Somewhere
the pen is always poised.

WILLIAM STAFFORD

At Bryant's Grave

A poet with a voice that is lost
lived here. Tangles the earth sends
grow over his paths. His wildfowl
cross and recross under jets
following their charts in the sky.

Lost people come here. They wander
as a gull grayly passes in the fog,
as the water gropes blindly, as the city
sends its rivers of traffic honking
their evening estuaries eastward.

A gray stone amid oaks, this lost
poet waits while a loud century
streams past. Translated by the years,
he abides with the sound of his words:
there is a tide underground.

REVA SHARON

Lines to William Cullen Bryant

This time I took the path
in the woods through
copper beech and tulip trees
. . . it has been a rainy season
and Indian pipes bloom everywhere
Now I am standing at the gate
blocked by a fallen tree
and gaze across the avenue
that bears your name
. . . the hum of traffic
is steady between
here and Cedarmere . . .
the rhythm of the century
that divides us

In June
the wild old rhododendron
was heavy with blossoms
A late spring breeze
was blowing through reeds
and willow branches
bending them down
the slopes toward your harbor
as I walked where once
your footsteps bent the grass
Later when I lay roses
on your grave

the shadow of the obelisk
fell across my shadow . . .

Wind-twined lines
of your poems
and the sound of leaf on leaf
echo in my ear . . .
In my hand I hold a heavy fruit
from your walnut tree
and seeds from uncut grass
cling to my hem
I look past your chosen home
over waters of the Sound
in the direction I am taking
and through the twilight
a silent wake ruffles
liquid bronze reflections

ROBYN SUPRANER

Midas' Daughter
    (after a walk through Cedarmere)

Who wished it?

Sky
Beaten and burnished
Glinting
Its gold cockade

Willow
Shouldering yellow
Epaulets, precious
And fringy?

Who?

Chestnut
Skirled and brassy
Clanging
In smelted metal

Gilt-fingered maple
Glazed
And whorled
Cast in holy simoleons

And

Oak leaves
Whole bowls of ingots
Beeches begetting
A dynasty of ormolu?

Who wished
This glistering canopy
This wrought peacock
This October?

Whose father?

LINDA PASTAN

Rereading "Thanatopsis"

In Roslyn, Long Island
where I didn't know
the poet had lived,
my uncle fresh from World War Two
built a ranch house
with an all electric
kitchen where I cooked eggs
for my small cousins and memorized
Bryant's poems for the eighth-grade teacher.
The only Waterfowl

I had seen
was drawn on the wing
of my uncle's fighter plane,
and I never guessed,
now that the war was won,
that "the last bitter hour"
was more than syllables
I had to learn
or could come so soon to tongue tie
even my razzle-dazzle uncle.

REVA SHARON

Winterscape – 1984

. . . and when the ills of life
Had chafed my spirit — I would wander forth
And seek the woods.
  A Winter Piece — William Cullen Bryant

Now arctic winds
are blowing out to sea
and snow falls
stilling the valley
Falls and collects on dark branches
settles on beds of pine needles
deepens over sleeping grass
falls on my unblinking lashes

buries mouldering leaves
Winter birds are silent in their nests
and queen bees are hibernating —
my breath is the only wing
floating through flakes
that fill my transient footprints
A mile from here the hawk is in the streets
In Lebanon the body count increases

Stalled in the calm
white eye of the storm
I am tempted
to lie down and feel
for the warm heart of the snow
leopard beating through
soft fur under the covered earth
Under the white and moss and lichen

where seeds of corn are waiting —
I want to stay
in shadows of trees
But where the road bends
close to the embankment
the splintered end
of a severed limb
thrusts darkly upward

WILLIAM HEYEN

Downriver

I
At the country auction, boxes of books. In one,
Bryant's *Poems*, a gilt-edged, false-leather parlor edition
losing its words, disbound, falling apart
even while I held it.

Under century-old backyard shagbark hickories
in the spread of full summer,
I stood reading "A Forest Hymn" for the first time
in twenty or thirty years.

Do you remember? You probably had it in high school,
as I did. Its hundred-eighteen lines
rocked all us little American scholars into oblivion.
Who cared about trees?

This was the day after a Russian pilot tracked a passenger jet,
locked in his missiles, and shot it down, killing 269.
I tried to imagine that many people in flames,
had counted the auction crowd to half that number.

Bryant rhapsodizes wildflowers growing at the roots
of huge trees. Each one, he says,
"With scented breath and look so like a smile,
Seems, as it issues from the shapeless mould,

An emanation of the indwelling Life,
A visible token of the upholding Love,
That are the soul of this great universe."
There's more in his hymn than heavenly flowers smiling,

but the desperate poet does blame all catastrophe on human pride
his forest could keep us from: "O God," he prays, "when thou
Dost scare the world with tempests, set on fire
The heavens with falling thunderbolts, or fill

The swift dark whirlwind that uproots the woods
And drowns the villages; when, at thy call,
Uprises the great deep and throws himself
Upon the continent, and overwhelms its cities,

Spare me and mine, nor let us need the wrath
Of the mad unchained elements to teach who rules them."
He ends by asking for that quiet wisdom to be found
under the emblematic trees in contemplation:

"Be it ours to meditate,
   In these calm shades, thy milder majesty,
   And to the beautiful order of thy works
   Learn to conform the order of our lives."

But I kept brooding the charred fuselage sinking into brine mud
with innocent dead, of limbs washed up on beaches.
I knelt to place the book back into its box.
A long time seemed to have passed.

II

The auction droned into evening, generations-deep possessions
knocked down for the dollars of inflation, spirited
across lawns from home, outbuildings, barns,
into cars and vans.

This was one of the old farmsteads along the Genesee
where the river still glides with Seneca apparitions
past graves of the first settlers. Who could have dreamed
the American city, a glass and steel skyline,

corporate limbs in a hundred countries?
But it was always there, born in the sewn brain-patterns
of homemade quilts, in the first Kodaks giving us back
to ourselves, in flails and scythes,

in pots mended by travelling tinkerers a hundred years before,
in anvils and ogee mirrors, in hand-ruled ledgers,
cast iron stoves, tin candle moulds, a trophy buck whose antlers
branched above this congregation,

in grains of the high-headboard oak beds
whose women bore those who worked this land, in the now
nondescript uniforms of three or four wars,
in shotguns, sheepskin coats, bridal gowns,

coarse overalls, a stereopticon, butter crocks, dovetailed dressers,
a rosewood Aeolian piano, corn shuckers, churns, apple peelers,
cabbage boards, blue-tinged canning jars, a loom,
a spinning wheel, a Currier & Ives of Sam Patch above the river,

a barrel of Depression glassware now fought for by dealers,
oval walnut frames of ancestral faces, redware, sheet music,
an Uncle Sam iron bank, a roll-top desk — the years
cascading forward with yearned-for objects as though

over the river's falls . . . . And then,
held up by the auctioneer for special admiration,
a single amethyst jack-in-the-pulpit bud vase, its cowl-
like spathe gleaming above dispersal & the emptiness of money . . . .

Did elms once clarify our streets with toothed translucent leaves?
Did we know God because the chestnut hillsides blossomed?
We pray, again, to invest things with meaning, to build a city
within our time but free from the terror of this new world.

III
The others have gone. Will you, now, stay here with me?
We will stand beside the river, watch stars hold still
in the flowing night water. In the same way,
we have come here from everywhere,

and from all time. We, our parents, theirs, theirs,
followed history, dumbly, or beguiled by it.
We were the ones in kitchens, fields, churches
of a thousand villages who heard the repeated dream

until we reached for it, or were handcuffed to it,
or driven toward it by famine, or slavers, or pogroms
of bayonet and flame. In 1834,
as he testifies in his *Narrative*, Frederick Douglass

prepared himself "for a final struggle which should decide
my fate, one way or the other." For Frederick,
for Susan B. Anthony in her and her sisters' life-long passional
against sexist greed and stupidity,

the same city still glows, downriver, over the treeline.
Lord of life and of all things, help us to know,
now, what our struggle is, its human forms
within objects within a world daily

more dangerous. Help us to know ourselves, the motives
of our most secret voices and gestures.
Stars in the river's water move, but stay,
as the river passes away, but stays. May we abide,

but build here the blessed city before we die . . . .
A slag-glass lamp, a book with Bryant's prayer, a two-handled
crosscut saw — let us look into one another's eyes
imagining flames, imagining love, and decide.

PHILIP APPLEMAN

After "Thanatopsis"

Black on black, from Maine to California:
the starshine is too precious now to keep.
I'm staking all my luck on one more morning
while everyone I love is sound asleep.

Suppose tomorrow were the last gold dawning,
painting the sky with rainbows of desire,
the last pale cloud, the last bright seagull soaring,
before the last red blossoming of fire —

the last green pine, the final blue wave breaking,
the long farewell in one last robin's song,
teaching us the truest kind of aching,
to love that well which we must leave 'ere long:

they'd feel it coming on in Kiev and China,
the poison rain, and murder in the snow,
the endless winter, birdless and benighted,
and sickness in the fields, where nothing grows.

From Paumanok it's black to the Pacific:
a nightbird says too late, you're in too deep.
Red telephones are jangling their dark traffic
while everyone I love is sound asleep.

PETER MICHELSON

Pantoum for William Cullen Bryant

Not everybody rhapsodizes Bill
these days. He contemplated death too young.
It was a freight that solemn time bore well.
Still, he craved an antique spirit's tongue,

and though he contemplated death too young
it's to the point that he admired trees
(while craving still an antique spirit's tongue).
He brought exotic fruits from overseas.

It's to the point that he admired trees,
configured in their groves a native hope.
Among exotic fruits from overseas,
Bartholdi's colossal Lady's colossal scope.

Configured in these groves of native hope
he heard the destined hum of multitudes
attending this colossal Lady's scope.
Her promise was pacific interludes.

He hymned the destiny of multitudes.
He saw it flooding from a cosmic urn —
the promise was pacific interludes.
But Black Hawk sensed more a mortal turn

in the cosmic hand that tipped the cosmic urn —
that is, a native thanatopsis
Black Hawk sensed, and not a comic turn. . . .
The Bitch delivered on her promiscuous promise.

So it goes, the native thanatopsis. . . .
Given the cosmic burn, what's so rare is
the Bitch delivered on her promiscuous promise.
So Bill rode horseback over Black Hawk's prairies.

Given comic turns, what's so rare is
that Bill inclined to call a *horse* a *steed*
and rode *airy undulations*, i.e. prairies,
but sat a saddle a hundred miles. Indeed,

he did incline to call a horse a steed
and fancied Mound Folk harnessed buffalo,
but he sat a saddle a hundred miles indeed.
Black Hawk went the way ancestors go.

Bill fancied Mound Folk harnessed buffalo.
It was a freight that solemn time bore well.
Black Hawk went the way ancestors go . . . .
Not everybody rhapsodizes Bill.

JARED CARTER

Raccoon Grove

> Let the mighty mounds
> That overlook the rivers, or that rise
> In the dim forest crowded with old oaks,
> Answer.
> *The Prairie* — William Cullen Bryant

To go, if there is time, to look at what
the land holds — some feature of their world
they wish to share, whether it be host
or stranger who comes up after the reading
and says, "If you're free tomorrow morning,
there's something that might interest you."
I find a way to meet them, to go see.

Every place has its secrets, its holes
and entryways into the earth, its shafts
abandoned and still burning underground,
its desert reaches: natural bridges spaced
through an entrenched meander; salt marsh
and bayou darkened by canvasback rising;
ridges stripped and gashed and left barren.

Always they want to visit wild places:
sail the catamaran across to Michigan's
archipelago, so far out the curvature
of earth hides everything but water and sky;
canoe down a spring-fed river in the Ozarks
through long tunnels of sycamores arching
smooth and white above their own reflections.

"I'm a landscape gardener," this man said,
after we had talked about the college
and all the good things it was doing.
"When the workshop's over tomorrow,
there's a place I'd like to take you to.
It's called Raccoon Grove. It's right
on the edge of where the prairie begins."

The next day we drove through the town.
"Germans built it," he explained, pointing
at the scroll-saw porches. "A station
on the Illinois Central. They used to raise
horses here. There was a lot of trading."
We stopped at a cemetery south of town:
all the old names were in black letter.

"My brother and I come here once a year,
   in the winter, after the first snowfall.
   We camp out, up there, along that ridge,
   the way we used to do, years ago.
   He's an architect now. We sit up
   most of the night and talk. Nurse the fire.
   Try to remember what we heard back then.

"Camped in Raccoon Grove every summer,
   too, in those days. An old man told us
   how he found a grave once, surrounded
   by logs, when he was a boy. It was
   an Indian princess's grave, he said,
   with four big cedar logs around it.
   We looked, but we never found anything.

"In the spring, after the first plowing,
   we used to wait for a rain, then start
   walking out across all this flat land.
   Imagine yourself a thousand years ago
   looking for a place to spend the night.
   Maybe over there. Go that way, even now,
   poke around, you'd find points and flints."

We parked and started into the grove.
   It was all red oak and shagbark hickory
   and no sound where we stepped, the leaves
   so thick, the creek so still. A warm day
   in late March, the equinox, too early
   for wildflowers, leaves beginning to show,
   stalks of unfolded fern springing up.

We followed the creek upstream. I saw
no litter anywhere, no sign of waste.
"It's not a park," he said. "The city
owns it. Everybody knows it's here.
Just a place to come and walk sometimes,
maybe camp for the night. Each of us
has old reasons for caring about it."

We crossed over and came to a high place
of bare earth and roots showing, stones
and sections of log ringing a fire pit.
It seemed a good place to rest. We sat
listening to the wind make the trees creak.
"The things you said last night," he began,
"or spoke, in your poems, about the earth —"

He fell silent for a moment. "I've been
all over this country. Alaska. Texas.
Lived with an uncle in Canada. Hitch-hiked
around Europe." I nodded. I'd done that too.
"Spent a lot of time in southwest England
and Wales, looking at those big stones."
I nodded again. I hadn't been there yet.

"Last night you talked about the mounds —
there," he said, pointing south, toward
the Wabash and the Ohio. "The old ones,
bordering the rivers, that go back a long way.
You had a grant to look at things like that."
"People are curious," I said, "they hope
someone might tell them what it means."

"And can you?" "No. Only that we're all
still looking, still trying to understand.
When there's time, I go out to those places,
those covered bridges, those brick sidewalks
hidden in the grass, that don't lead anywhere.
I read the old writers, too, the forgotten ones,
those who wrote about how that world looked.

"It doesn't matter if they're not remembered.
They saw the same things then that we see now.
It doesn't change that much — not the trees,
not the animals, not the sound of the birds.
You can walk out onto one of those mounds
all by yourself, in that stillness, and know
it's unchanged. Same river down there, flowing."

It was time to go. We walked toward the car.
"I don't read much," he said. "I know green things.
Once in a while, out like this, I'll see trees
that look as though someone had planted them
in a straight line. When an old tree leans,
sometimes it will sucker out along one side.
When it finally goes down, all those branches

become new trees, standing in a row, growing
out of the old one. You can read them
like an arrow blazed there, an inscription
for those who come after." "For those,"
I said, "who take the time to look, who want
to see." "Yes." We drove back to town.
The sun was still high when we shook hands.

ALBERT F. McLEAN

*William Cullen Bryant
at the Tomb of Napoleon Bonaparte*
(May, 1853)

Look, look, noble Yankee, upon this alien magnificence.
Your meditating eye browses among the marbles, bronzes,
And the canopy that will shroud Napoleon's still fierce heart.
In the throng of the devout, you press to the balustrade.
You witness the sarcophagus, open and empty, awaiting
    its conqueror.
Choir voices that float in the chill nave,
Chant an anthem of peace transcendent, of victory over death.
But your analogy slices through this "glittering polish,"
This artifice of adoration. You recall a view at Sakkara —
The open chests of porphyry, in which an ancient race
Had entombed another alien relic,
The bones of Egypt's sacred ox.
Each nation honors, so you contemplate,
Life in death's form, immortalized.

Which, you ask, to New English sensibility,
Is nobler of the two, Bonaparte or ox?

The crowd presses on, down to the crypt beyond,
To the great Court of the *Invalides*,
To the massive bronze statues, their emblems
Of domination, globe and sceptre, proudly grasped.
You see and scorn the lavish symbols of war,
Prowess, glory, conquest, and human slaughter.

Tourist Cullen Bryant, you record your images in prose
Bare of ornament, precise in its detail,
Faithful to the readers of the *Evening Post*.
You are a solid purveyor of taste and judgement.
Vineyards, fountains, Alpine vistas, and the ruins
Of antiquity are the substance of your dispatches.
Yet you also depict the newly drowned on view
In the morgue in Paris, macabre graveyards
Littered with human bones,
And some fascinating lunatic asylums.
Your literate light is cast into dark, forbidden places.
You traffic, after all, in vision, so you write
Of paintings, painters, galleries and exhibitions,
Transposing from canvas to a printed page the substance
Of your vision — story, sentiment, and moral symbolism.

As when you studied three paintings by Delaroche,
Portraying Napoleon at stages of his life's way.
Youthful "Napoleon Crossing the Alps," confident and resolute.
Then the self-satisfied Napoleon: "Europe at his feet," you said.
And last the tragic denouement, "Napoleon at Fontainebleau" —
Disheveled, despairing, given over to a "fixed, sullen gaze."
You confirmed your own gray view of human history.

Sepulchres for a sacred ox's bones and the heart of Bonaparte?
At least Egypt paid homage to a useful tribe of animals,
You write, just as Yankee Ben proposed the wild turkey
As the national bird. Cling to peace and daily work.
Distill the stuff of carnage and cataclysm, gore and glory,
Death and dementia into a poetic of sentiment.
History, after all, is story — the legend left from long ago.

RICHARD ELMAN

Autumn at Mill Pond

(for William Cullen Bryant and Walt Whitman)

The honeyed Fall
as thick as dew
mud sweet and
heavy laid
across this earth
is sure to end.

Such leafy stews,
berry red leaves,
and hedges browned
with redness will,
at kill frost time,
crisp and sere,
then disappear.

Stick time comes
as cold as
green was green,
and brittle.
Filled with late sun
yellow berries
bear up against
a chill that rises
like subtle fog.

The lawn sinks
down to stone.
The final heat
is more intense
for being only
Indian summer
icy at dawn.

GRACE VOLICK

Bryant's Vision

How much we must envy your
unbroken look at the forest
rising like the limbs
of a new country — your gift
under its giant shade
to see in the trackless dark
cathedrals of light.

WILLIAM STAFFORD

A Wedge of Oak

At Bryant's grave someone had chainsawed down an old oak. By counting rings in a wedge from the trunk I found that the tree had been living when Bryant was living there. This wedge I carried with me, and over the next few weeks it stayed on my desk and led to some notes, to many wandering speculations.

Just after that visit I find scattered phrases — "a poet with a lost voice . . . his waterfowl . . . his grave. . . ." And days later an odd sequence about trees in my daily journal links back to the oak wedge, to the Bryant house with its paths overgrown and tangled: —

The shadow a tree has inside itself
begins to touch my shadow. My shadow
sways. Into the forest a whisper
vanishes — less than the shadows, less
than silence, but having devoured them.

Trees have swallowed their shadows. Through all
the northland moonlight scours for silver.
Even smallest branches hold still;
voices have died. Where a voice will come,
a great brightness begins.

They have retreated — the trees — from where
they once were. Open to the sky, this place
discovers its reason.

So many times the open trees have invited me
and a river, coming from nowhere, has appeared,
splashing for sunlight, and gone by. . . .

ABOUT THE POETS

PHILIP APPLEMAN is a novelist, historian, editor of a collection of essays on Darwin, and poet who is a Distinguished Professor of English at Indiana University. His four poetry collections include *Open Doorways* and, most recently, *Darwin's Ark*.

JARED CARTER, a midwestern writer who lives in Indianapolis, won the Walt Whitman Award (Academy of American Poets) for his *Work, for the Night Is Coming*. His subsequent collections are *Pincushion's Strawberry* and *Fugue State*.

VINCE CLEMENTE is Professor of English at Suffolk Community College where he teaches a course in Long Island Poets and the Landscape. He coedited the anthology *Paumanok Rising* and has published poetry collections titled *Snow Owl above Stony Brook Harbor* and *Broad Bill off Conscience Bay*.

RICHARD EBERHART, Emeritus Professor of several universities, has served as Poet Laureate of New Hampshire. He has won the Bollingen Prize, the Pulitzer Prize, and, for his *Collected Poems*, the National Book Award. His latest of 25 collections is *The Long Reach: New and Uncollected Poems 1948–1984*, and a selection of his prose is titled *Of Poets and Poetry*.

RICHARD ELMAN is a novelist, short-story writer, journalist, and poet who lives in Stony Brook, Long Island, the setting of "Autumn at Mill Pond." He has taught at the University of Pennsylvania and has poetry volumes titled *Homage to Fats Navarro* and *In Chontales*.

PAUL ENGLE founded the Iowa Writers Workshop, the first in the U.S., and the International Writing Program of the University of Iowa. He edited the anthology *Midland* and several volumes of O. Henry Prize Stories, and has to his credit many poetry collections, including *American Child* and the recent *Engle Country: Poems*.

WILLIAM HEYEN is a Professor of English at SUNY Brockport where he teaches American literature and creative writing. He edited the anthologies *American Poets in 1976* and *The Generation of 2000*, & his major collections are *Long Island Light: Poems and a Memoir* and *Erika: Poems of the Holocaust*.

JOHN HOLLANDER, Professor of English at Yale, has won the Bollingen Prize. He has written of poetic form in *Vision and Resonance* and *Rhyme's Reason* and his poetry collections include a selected poems titled *Spectral Emenations* and *Powers of Thirteen*.

AARON KRAMER, Professor of English at Dowling College, discusses the poetry of W.C.B. at length in *The Prophetic Tradition in American Poetry*. A translator of Heine, Rilke, and Ingeborg Bachmann, he has edited the anthology *On Freedom's Side* and published several collections, including *On the Way to Palermo* and *The Burning Bush: Poems and Other Writings 1940–1980*.

ALBERT F. MCLEAN, Vice President and Academic Dean of Point Park College in Pittsburgh, is the author of the Twayne United States Author Series *William Cullen Bryant*. His poems have appeared in various journals and have been selected for inclusion in the Borestone Best Poems of the Year series.

PETER MICHELSON teaches in the writing program at the University of Colorado. His poetry collections include *Pacific Plainsong*, a cycle about the conflict between the whites and Indians of the Northwest, and, most recently, *When the Revolution Really*.

ROBERT MORGAN, a native of North Carolina, the setting for many of his poems, teaches English at Cornell University. His five collections include *Red Owl* and *Groundwork*.

LINDA PASTAN lives in Potomac, Maryland. Her collections include *Waiting for my Life* and *P.M./A.M.: New and Selected Poems*, nominated for the 1982 American Book Award in Poetry.

REVA SHARON is the founding editor of *The Cedarmere Review*. Her poems have appeared in *West Hills Review, New Traditions*, and *Blood to Remember: American Poets on the Holocaust*.

WILLIAM JAY SMITH, former Consultant in Poetry to the Library of Congress, lives in the "Bryant Cottage" in Cummington, Mass. Translator of poetry from several languages, author of books for children, he has published a number of collections, including *Journey to the Dead Sea*, and his selected poems, *The Traveler's Tree*.

WILLIAM STAFFORD, who taught for thirty years at Lewis and Clark College in Portland, Oregon, has served as Consultant in Poetry to the Library of Congress. He won the National Book Award in Poetry for *Traveling Through the Dark* and titled his collected poems *Stories That Could Be True*.

ROBYN SUPRANER lives in Roslyn Harbor, a short walk from Cedarmere. She has published many children's books, several of which have won awards. Her poems have appeared in *Ploughshares*, *The Massachusetts Review*, and the *Beloit Poetry Journal*.

GRACE VOLICK teaches contemporary literature and creative writing at Long Island University, C. W. Post Campus. Her poems have appeared in the *Chicago*, *Antioch*, and *West Coast Poetry* Reviews.

RICHARD WILBUR, the distinguished poet, translator, and editor whose awards include the Pulitzer Prize, the National Book Award, and the Bollingen Prize, lives not far from the Bryant Homestead in Cummington, Mass. His collections include *Walking to Sleep* and *The Mind-Reader*.

NORBERT KRAPF is a Professor of English at Long Island University, C. W. Post Campus, where he has taught since 1970. He holds the Ph.D. in English and American Literature from the University of Notre Dame, was a U.S. exchange teacher at West Oxfordshire Technical College, and served as senior Fulbright lecturer in American poetry at the University of Freiburg, Germany. His scholarly articles, reviews, translations, and poems have appeared widely in journals, little magazines, and anthologies, including *American Scholar*, *Walt Whitman Review*, *Poetry*, *Poetry Now*, *New Letters*, and *Anthology of Magazine Verse and Yearbook of American Poetry*. For three of his six poetry collections, *Arriving on Paumanok*, *Lines Drawn from Dürer*, and *Heartwood*, he received a Trustees' Award for Scholarly Achievement 1984 from Long Island University. His translations of early poems by Rainer Maria Rilke, *Shadows on the Sundial*, and a collection of materials about the German heritage of his native southern Indiana, *Stories They Wanted to Tell*, are forthcoming. He lives with his wife and two children in an old house in Roslyn, where William Cullen Bryant had a home for 35 years.

PRINTER'S NOTE

IT IS FITTING that *Under Open Sky,* a reappraisal of the works and stature of William Cullen Bryant, once regarded as America's pre-eminent poet, was designed & printed in "Stone House," a dwelling he built 115 or more years ago for members of his family. His own house, "Cedarmere," where he wrote some of the poems that are discussed in this book, still stands, a few minutes' walk distant, on a slope overlooking Hempstead Bay.

The editor and contributor to this book, Norbert Krapf, like Bryant a poet of nature, brought together the distinguished group of poets whose contributions make this an important enhancement of our understanding of Bryant.

John De Pol, an acknowledged master of contemporary wood engraving, expresses his sensitive appreciation of the nineteenth-century poet's feeling for nature in seventeen memorable engravings that dance with light and shadow.

Since the edition published by The Stone House Press was limited to 185 copies, it is pleasing that this trade edition of *Under Open Sky* is now published by Fordham University Press, already the publishers of four volumes of the ongoing series *The Letters of William Cullen Bryant,* edited by William Cullen Bryant II.

M. A. G.

COLOPHON

Under Open Sky was designed by M. A. Gelfand, and printed by him with assistance from Jim Ricciardi and Lynn Peterson at The Stone House Press. It was set in Monotype Emerson at Out of Sorts Letter Foundery, Mamaroneck, New York, with hand composition at the Press. He has provided the reproduction proofs from which this edition of 1,000 copies has been printed on Mohawk Superfine paper.